1

7:15 Am
Spring Dental
Claremore
504 Lynn Riggs
Blvd.
Claremore Ok
918-283- 7377

er

.

ough Stuff of
tion

No Matter What...

Karla Marie Williams
Copyright 2020
ISBN 9781081753986

Publisher: BeBold Publishing
Author: Karla Marie Williams

Contributing Writers:
Heidi Senior
Tiana Hawver
Agnes Tucker

Editor: Kerrie McLoughlin

Beta Readers:
Regina Traylor
Carrie Burrows
Lisa Faber

Language: English
Printed in the U.S.A.
First Edition

"Karla Marie Williams has what every foster and adoptive mother needs most: courage and faith. In NO MATTER WHAT, she exposes the journey of parenting a child from trauma and the hope that we all cling to in the process. Her transparency in sharing her own traumas and how they impacted her parenting makes this book essential for second mothers. You will find so much comfort and useful advice here. I am so grateful for this book and the way it gives voice to my journey!"

Jodi Jackson Tucker
Author, Child Advocate
&
International Director
of Orphan Sunday/Stand Sunday
www.orphansunday.org

Table of Contents

"It is never too late to develop an open and trusting relationship with your child. It takes humility and patience, but it can be done. There is no better day than the present to begin."

Karla Marie Williams

Dedication

I dedicate this book to the late Dr. Karyn Purvis. It was her work, research, and wisdom that helped me through the darkest and most confusing days of parenting my children. I have learned so much from her writings and teachings. She has helped me and other desperate parents reach their kids and help them along a journey of healing. I met her one time at a conference and her warm eyes and soft-spoken wisdom comforted me and gave me the confidence that I could be a catalyst of healing for my kids.

Many people cannot say they have impacted generations. Dr. Karyn Purvis impacted generations to come. For this, I am forever grateful.

Introduction
Inspired by My Children

This book and my career were greatly inspired by my children. I am not a social worker, psychologist, or therapist. I am a mom who is passionate about advocating for children who have been marginalized and pushed aside by society and traumatized at the hands of adults. After adopting my first three children, I realized how unprepared and clueless I was about the needs and care required for children that had experienced horrible traumatic events in their early lives.

I have spent many years traveling throughout the US, Africa, Asia, and Latin America. Through my organization, iSpeak4KidsGlobal, I inspire and train foster parents, child advocates, social workers, and clergy on trauma competent care for kids. I have had the pleasure of praying with, coaching, and helping parents through very tough times. I know from my personal and professional experience that a trauma competent and equipped family can make a major difference in a child's life.

In this book, I will take you through the career that took me by surprise, my foster care adoption story, and everything that I have learned first-hand and professionally as a consultant to families in crisis across the globe.

I will share with you some painful moments and many victories I have celebrated as I parent and nurture my children. My story as a healing agent and trauma competent parent is continually unfolding. I am not perfect, but my desire is to always be perfected and do better as I learn and grow alongside my precious kids.

There are plenty of books on the market to inspire you to foster or adopt. They are necessary. My purpose for writing this book is completely different. I want to answer those hard questions like, "Why is my child hoarding food?", "Why does my child smear his feces?", "Are we the only family that deals with these things?" No, you are not. Take comfort in knowing that there are answers here to help you make sense of things and become the healing agent that you desire to be for your children. Every child that has experienced life in foster care or an institution has not had all of the challenges mentioned in this book. However, they are extremely common, and many families struggle to help their kids.

Throughout this book, I will refer to circumstances and challenges that my children and other families have had to contend with as a result of the response to early trauma. I will not disclose names and identities out of respect for my children and the other families mentioned in this book. Their stories are their own to tell.

My prayer for the readers of this body of work is that they will be enlightened, inspired, moved to change, and fully equipped to compassionately guide the children in their care. You may be a foster parent, adoptive parent, teacher, social worker, or you may work with at-risk or traumatized youth. This book is an open door to help you understand the raw and very real effects of trauma on the children you love and work with. I pray you are ready to stick it out and walk through the tough stuff with your kids NO MATTER WHAT…

l

"If there is a cause worth fighting for it's this:
Children Belong in Families!"

Nicole Skellenger

Chapter 1
Back to the Beginning

*I*t was November 15, 2005. It was cold outside, and I had just returned from lunch and made it back to my office. I was dragging and knowing that things had to be better than this. I had so many desires and dreams burning inside of me. Even though I had reached my career goals up to this point, it was not enough. I hated being stuck in an office and doing the same tasks over and over again. Don't get me wrong, I was good at what I did. Human Resources and organizing systems were my things. I even enjoyed the people that I worked with. I was just uneasy. Unsatisfied. Unhappy. I couldn't even tell you why.

My discontent goes back five years to December 2000. Tom and I had been trying to have a baby for two years. I wanted nothing more than to hold a baby in my arms and be a mother. We finally found out that we were expecting, and it was surreal. Shortly after finding out we were going to be parents, we miscarried. This miscarriage was the first of seven miscarriages over the course of many years.

The most painful moment as we were trying to conceive and carry a baby full-term came in the summer of 2003. I had sustained the pregnancy until fourteen weeks. We were so excited. It was the longest pregnancy at that point. One night while lying in bed, I heard and felt a pop. The bed was wet, and I knew exactly what was happening.

"Please, baby, stay with me," I remember saying as I rolled out of the bed and went to the bathroom. It was there in that bathroom that I cried out to God, and called my husband's name as I delivered an extremely premature baby. I had to gather my things and get in the car and head to the hospital with the baby in my arms, tiny, lifeless, and hardly resembling a healthy newborn. They whisked me in one direction and the baby in another, as my husband stood helpless and emotional in the hospital hallway. The last thing I remember before passing out was a large woman aggressively pushing on my stomach in a panic. There were a few more attempts at pregnancy after this baby, and a couple of surprise pregnancies that ended the same way.

No career climb or accomplishment could quench my desire to simply be a mom. It was all I could think about. All I read about. It was quite an obsession really. I didn't know how to be happy. I didn't understand how one could be happy in such circumstances. My husband was fed up with the emotional turmoil of the empty attempts and the toll it was taking on my body. Eventually we decided our goal was to be parents and there was more than one way to do that.

We thought about a private adoption. The cost was not feasible for us, and my heart was not comfortable with that decision. We had learned about many families choosing international adoption; however, this cost was astronomical and the travel involved wasn't something our current jobs would allow. After researching many different avenues, we landed in a state agency to inquire about foster care adoption.

When the phone rang on November 15, 2005, it seemed like just another call about paperwork from the agency. Our foster/adoption worker was on the other end.

She asked me if I was sitting down. This had to be big. I couldn't let myself get excited. I was afraid to hope because of all the loss and pain we had experienced already.

"Are you sitting down?" asked Michele.

"Yes. What is this about?" I asked, curious and slightly nervous.

"This is THE call!" she replied with excitement in her voice.

"Oh my God. Oh my God. Oh my God!" I kept repeating as I put her on hold to close my office door.

"Karla, I have two sweet babies I want you to consider. They are siblings. She is three years old and he is two years old."

I barely heard anything else that she said after that. I was in shock. I couldn't speak or respond. It is happening. I am going to be a mom. FINALLY! She continued to give me details. She emailed me their profiles and pictures. She planned to come over that evening to discuss it more and bring more pictures for us.

Tom had taken the day off work. I called him a few times without an answer. He finally picked up the phone, groggy and half asleep.

"Hi, Daddy!" I said.

"Hi!" he replied, not getting my joke.

"Hello, DADDY!" I said again.

"Wait, what?" he answered, as he was finally catching on.

I went on to tell him the amazing news and he was excited but still too groggy to grasp what was happening. Was he dreaming? The rest of the workday was a bust. The whole building knew the good news by the end of the workday. I was floating and instantly wanted to start nesting and shopping.

We met them on December 10, 2005. She was the spunkiest little three-year-old I had ever met. He was a chatty and intellectual two-year-old who was mature beyond his years. We were in love!

We spent the next two months visiting and spending time with them in their foster home and bringing them to our home to get adjusted. On February 14, 2006, they finally came home permanently. We became parents that day.

"I couldn't speak or respond. It is happening. I am going to be a mom."

We had quite the fast-paced lifestyle when we brought our children home. We quickly realized that things had to change. I enjoyed being home with them. However, I was surrounded by friends and family who were high achievers in the workplace and I secretly longed for that.

The transition into motherhood was not as smooth as I had hoped. Bonding with my babies took more effort than I expected. I didn't quite understand why. We adjusted and put our all into parenting these little people.

After three months of the kids being home, I began looking for another job. I landed a job that I absolutely loved, and it was the next step in my career as a Human Resources professional. I was confident and happy. Motherhood was amazing and I was rocking it at work. Things could not have been more perfect. Who said you cannot have it all?

July 24, 2006

"This is Karla. How can I help you?"

"Hello, Karla, this is Dawn from the agency."

"Hello. How are you?" I replied.

"Great. We have some news for you. Your children have a baby brother that was born two days ago and there is no one here to pick him up."

"Wait, excuse me?" I said in disbelief.

She repeated herself. I told her that I needed to talk to my husband and that I would call her back first thing in the morning. In the meantime, he would go to a foster home. It took a while to determine if we could indeed do this. After being childless for eight years of our marriage, could we really handle two toddlers and a newborn all at once?

It took a few months for our foster license and home study to be updated. We were finally able to bring him home. We were in love. I was Super Woman. A working mom with three children under the age of three. A minister with demanding responsibilities. Once again, I was rocking it… or so it appeared. I was trying to do it all, and eventually I wore myself down.

I was falling apart at the seams. Having three children in daycare was burning a huge hole in our pockets and it was starting to make no sense at all. My three-year-old was running the daycare daily, against the owner's wishes – she was bossy and out of control. My two-year-old was dealing with asthma and challenges with anger. My newborn was on a heart monitor, which caused me daily anxiety. I had to leave work at least two days a week to check on the well-being of my kids. It was taking a toll on our family, all while I was trying to remain dedicated to my job and role as a minister.

January of 2007, after doing the math, we decided that being home with our children was the best choice for me. It was hard transitioning from career woman to stay-at-home-mom. However, like I do everything else, I threw myself into my new role and made it enjoyable. After a while, I was thrilled to be home and spend those early years with them. I cherished those park days and never-ending picnics. We intentionally slowed our entire lifestyle down to benefit our children and things began to go smoothly.

As we adjusted our fast-paced lifestyle, we began to enjoy life and each other much more. We began to notice behaviors and responses to everyday things that would throw our children into a complete tailspin.

We did not understand what we were experiencing. Out of ignorance, we tried all kinds of traditional parenting methods. None of them worked. It was quite a blow to my self-esteem as a mom that I could not help my kids with their struggles. Remember, we went into this situation because we wanted to be parents. We had no idea what trauma looked like or how it affected our little ones' brains and their outlook on life.

After reading a few books and talking to other adoptive parents, I started researching trauma. I began digging for answers so that I could be the best mom possible to my kids. Although we noticed some results of their early trauma, it was not nearly as dramatic as the stories I was hearing in the books and videos I watched.

The behavior we were experiencing with my oldest child led me to investigate homeschooling. This later led to homeschooling all of my children.

At that time in my life, I really did think that love was all my children needed to thrive. There was so much I had to learn.

Seven years and two moves later, we decided that we wanted to adopt more children. We knew it would have to be at least two children, because we did not want a fourth child to feel left out due to the other children being siblings. We settled on two children until I had a dream about a sibling group of three. My dreams have always been vivid, accurate, and a way for God to talk to me. We discussed it, and three it was!

In the spring of 2012, we called our agency that we used for the first three children. We spent that summer updating our home study and preparing our home and lifestyle for another big transition.

On February 14, 2013, we got a phone call about three children, ages six, five, and three years old. Of course, just like the first time, we were the only family at the agency crazy enough to actually request three children at once. They shared their names and emailed us their file for more information. We knew this was it.

We dropped the other kids off at my mother-in-law's and headed east for an hour to meet with what we thought were two social workers. To our surprise, we were in a room with our social worker, the children's social worker, the children's lawyer, a CASA representative, the agency director, and two state officials on the teleconference line. Why in the world did we need all of these people involved to explain our future children's case? We were about to find out!

"Remember, we went into this situation because we wanted to be parents. We had no idea what trauma looked like or how it affected our little ones' brains and outlook on life."

The children's case was explained to us in the order of the case file. I felt like everyone in the room was waiting for us to walk out and bail. We remained calm and poised, as we usually are. They explained the five homes they had been in and why they were continually moved.

Next came a list of behaviors that resulted from the trauma and experiences they had had. We still were not moved. It came to a point where they asked us if we really felt like we could handle this trio. One child in particular was a topic of concern, as the trauma and behavior were the most extreme. The room was full of everyone vested in making sure this move was the last and final move for them.

We were not moved. When you believe that God is leading you, you can walk in a confidence that many don't understand. I, myself, had been through much of what the children had been through. I felt confident in being able to raise them in a happy and healthy environment. After everyone in the room agreed that this was a good move for the children, we began planning a transition strategy to minimize any negative effects on the kids.

We had moved away from the city where our original agency was. For this reason, we had to travel an hour twice a week to visit our babies. Like any honeymoon period, it was delightful, as we got to witness their cute little personalities and quirks. We knew that there might be rough days ahead, but for right now we wanted to be present and enjoy this time with them.

On March 24, 2013, I became a mother of six children under the age of 10. I welcomed the chaos and all the energy. It was a dream come true. When Tom and I dated, one thing we had in common was that we wanted six children. We had no idea it would come through foster care adoption, but it happened.

We stopped all of our homeschool activity and focused solely on gelling as a family of eight. There were some days that were overwhelming due to the logistics of having a large family and other days that I felt like a domestic goddess.

A few months into our new normal, things began to change rapidly. The most dramatic of the issues was how my child, who used to be the baby of the family, now had three children younger than him. His ability to navigate from baby to big brother was a really rough road.

The older children seemed to be happy and adjusting well. I don't think that I was paying enough attention to know for sure. I later came to the conclusion that this was not the case at all. My oldest daughter was not doing well with another girl on her turf. My oldest son, who was the quietest one and least likely to share his feelings, recalls moments of bitterness as well.

We were dealing with some textbook issues when it comes to trauma. Then we began to deal with some not-so-typical behaviors that knocked us off our feet. Our new babies had suffered so much tragedy in their lives, and it was showing at every turn.

Yet, we were committed to it all. We did not just sign up for the easy days. We signed up for it all, and we were determined to educate ourselves and advocate for the needs of our kids NO MATTER WHAT…

Beautiful Moments

Hearing the little footsteps of six children in my home
after years of heartache and multiple miscarriages
was a beautiful moment.

What I Have Learned

I learned that children are children. Take away the trauma
and you have children full of dreams and laughter, just
like any other child.

Prayer

Lord, give us the compassion, wisdom, and patience as
we embark upon fostering and/or adopting the children
you desire to be a part of our family for a moment, or a
lifetime. Help us navigate this foreign process with grace
and peace.

In Jesus' Name,
Amen

"A child born to another woman calls me Mommy. The magnitude of that tragedy and the depth of that privilege are not lost on me."

Jody Landers

Chapter 2
Ruined Perfection

Perfect Parent

*O*h, the parent I dreamed I would be. The vision I had long before I had the privilege of being a parent was absolute perfection. I would do and say all the right things. I would be the Stepford wife and mom. I would know what to say and do at all the right times.

Sadly, I crashed and burned so fast after becoming a mom. I have learned over the years to give myself grace on those difficult days when I cannot seem to get anything right. Those days when I feel like I am the worst mom in the world, God speaks to me and encourages me that I am not. He lets me know how to make things right and try again tomorrow. It becomes easier and easier to accept my frailties as a human being. I don't think there is a mother alive who is not her own worst critic.

Parenting has brought me to my knees day after day. I was clueless, especially in the area of trauma. I didn't know what my kids needed, and I didn't know where to find it. There were very few people around me who were familiar with trauma. I found myself trying to pretend to be the perfect mom out of fear. What would everyone think if they knew I wasn't a perfect mom? I later found out that other moms felt the same way and my fear dissipated and turned into hope. Hope that I can keep getting better and showing up for my kids NO MATTER WHAT…

Perfect Kid

There is the perfection that you expect from yourself and then there is that "dream child" that you always wanted. The obedient, polite, well-behaved, adorable little Einstein that was going to change the world in his lifetime. We all start out in parenthood with those dreams. Much of it will be true of your children as you raise them, but it may not be the package you were anticipating. Whether your children are biological or adopted, they are individuals created by God with a purpose all their own. They have strengths, talents, weaknesses, successes, seasons of greatness, and times of great struggle. They are absolutely amazing.

"Whether your children are biological or adopted, they are individuals created by God with a purpose all their own."

You cannot be so bent on who and what your child is going to be based on your vision, that they are not allowed to grow, fail, or be themselves. Children who have been through unspeakable tragedies and trauma may not present as that gem upfront. Armed with compassion and trauma knowledge, you can help them toward healing and begin to see that amazing person they have the potential to be. Underneath the anger, questionable behavior, choices, and fear is a kid who needs you to love and nurture who God created them to be. It is unfair to a child to expect them to live up to your idea of a perfect kid, especially when they are working through trauma and behaviors that wreak havoc on their self-esteem.

After I started advocating for kids in foster care, I had a lot of people paying attention to my new family, many of whom had never considered foster care or adoption before observing our family come together. While some were well intentioned, many were not. One such encounter makes me sick to my stomach as I rehearse it in my mind.

I got a phone call from the assistant of a prominent person in my circle. The assistant asked me how to go about adopting a baby with the least amount of trouble. I thought they were asking for themselves. It turns out they were asking for their boss. The first red flag was the fact that anyone serious about making a positive impact in a child's life should not put the investigation off on a second party. Before I could get a word in edgewise, the assistant went on to give me a list of the perfect kid. The child must be a boy with a light complexion and curly hair. Her boss did not want anything to do with the parents and would not consider a child where drugs and alcohol were involved. I was polite until she was done. After we hung up, I had tears in my eyes. I wanted to scream, "THAT IS NOT HOW THIS WORKS. THAT IS NOT HOW ANY OF THIS WORKS!" This is not a person who should be fostering or adopting a child. She wanted a robot, a doll, but certainly not a child. If she could request the gene pool, she probably would have. Needless to say, I never followed up with her or embarrassed myself by giving her the phone number to my beloved agency.

Before we even considered adoption, we lost several babies to miscarriage. The pain that came with that was excruciating. In the meantime, everyone around me was starting a family the old-fashioned way. I celebrated them, planned showers, bought gifts, but I was slowly dying inside. Nothing could dull the sting of the repeated struggle to become a mom. I had to take time and deal with my feelings and recognize what was going to be important when we chose to adopt. My children would need all of me. They should not need to live up to my vision of the perfect kid.

"Once upon a time, I was the perfect parent. Then I had children. The End."
Unknown

When a couple is considering adoption after the loss of a child or miscarriage, I have very important advice for them. Heal first. Do not go into adoption to heal the loss of a child or to replace a child. That is unfair to everyone involved. Deal with your emotions regarding your loss and come to terms with the tragedy before moving forward with adoption.

If the perfection you expected from yourself or your child has been squashed and ruined, you are just where God wants you to be: a place of new beginnings where you can rely on Him to mold you into the parent he has called you to be. Simultaneously, he will give you the wisdom and direction to be a healing agent for your children and guide them through the challenges and victories ahead. NO MATTER WHAT, you must stay connected to God to be able to effectively help your child.

Beautiful Moments

When I recognized that there was no such thing as a perfect mom, it was a beautiful moment for me. I was then able to give myself grace and work hard to change and grow with my kids.

What I Have Learned

I have learned that children need a parent who is committed to them more than a parent who is perfect. They want to know you will be there on both good and bad days.

Prayer

Dear Lord, help me to look at myself through your eyes so that I can become the parent you desire me to be. Let me also look at my child through your eyes, perfectly designed and precious in your sight. Let us walk in grace and forgiveness for one another as we walk this road together.

In Jesus' Name,
Amen

"Nourishing myself is a joyful experience and I am worth the time spent on my healing."

Louise Hay

Chapter 3
Address the Mess

*I*n my book, *Let Go!*, I share so many of the life experiences that shape my adult fears, anxiety, walls, and attitudes. I was a mess, y'all!

I was a minister of the gospel. I truly thought I had dealt with and experienced healing in the areas of my life that would be problematic roadblocks. I had not. Instead, I had figured out how to push the feelings down deep in a long-term state of denial.

It all culminated into gaining lots of weight, episodes of internal rage, and depression. After we adopted our children, those nasty little things started showing up all over the place. Feelings, perspectives, and behavior that I swore was NOT ME. Only it was ME. It was the part of me I had suppressed and not dealt with.

"Once you recover from being triggered, the most helpful question you can ask yourself is, 'When have I felt this way before? And before that? And before that?' Deep triggers are connected to pre-birth and early life experiences. Bring the subconscious to the conscious."
Post Institute

Dealing with your own stuff is important so it does not interfere with your ability to parent compassionately. One such example of this was my suffering from multiple miscarriages and living life in the fast lane to avoid feeling anything. I was afraid to get quiet, slow down, and acknowledge that I was in so much pain. I had become numb to the idea of being a mother.

When we began to consider adoption after so much loss, I was terrified that I would not allow myself to bond with a child for fear of losing them. I had to allow myself to grieve for many reasons. First of all, grief is healthy. We were not meant to carry all that pain. God wants to relieve us of that inner turmoil when we are willing to hand it over to him. Secondly, I did not want my fears, anxieties, and lack of healing to reflect in the expectations and parenting of the children we would bring into our home. That would be unfair and would jeopardize the bond and relationship with my new children.

Whatever that thing is for you, let it go. Let God have it. Free yourself of those childhood and adulthood issues that affect you today. I guarantee they affect how you parent and relate to your children. Work on that.

Secondary Trauma
According to the *Psychiatric Times*, secondary trauma is defined as indirect exposure to trauma through a firsthand account or narrative of a traumatic event.

Vicarious Trauma
According to the American Counseling Association, vicarious trauma is the emotional residue of exposure that counselors have from working with people as they are hearing their trauma stories and become witnesses to the pain, fear, and terror that trauma survivors have endured.

The difference between secondary trauma and vicarious trauma is that secondary trauma can happen suddenly, in **one session,** while vicarious trauma is a response to an **accumulation of exposure** to the pain of others (Figley, 1995). The symptoms of secondary trauma are nearly identical to those of vicarious trauma.

In the beginning, we were unaware of what to expect with our children. The adoption process was seamless, truly something from a fairy tale from our point of view. A couple that tried to become parents for years were suddenly parents, and they all rode off into the sunset.

"First of all, grief is healthy. We were not meant to carry all that pain. God wants to relieve us of that inner turmoil when we are willing to hand it over to him."

NOT SO FAST! We forgot there were little people with a previous life, pain, separation, abuse, trauma, feelings, and confusion in our arms. This was not a fairy tale at all. From their little perspectives, this ball of confusion could very well be a nightmare.

We learned very quickly that there was a lot that we did not know. We had to educate ourselves in order to explain what we were experiencing with our new babies.

We have dedicated our time to educating ourselves and others on trauma competency. We are continually learning what we need to know for our own parenting journey and as much as we can to help other parents in the trenches.

Over the years, we have taken the brunt of our children's anger, pain, and blame. We have experienced both physical and psychological stress from the behavior associated with our children's trauma.

I can attest to times that my kids have behaved in such a way that triggered my own childhood issues. That is when I knew that I had a lot of inner work to do myself.

As a mom, I suffered post-adoption depression after the adoption of both sibling groups. I don't attribute it to the children, or fault them at all. It is attributed to the hype and excitement, expectations, and emotions involved in the process that are such a contrast to the reality that follows.

"As a mom, I suffered post-adoption depression after the adoption of both sibling groups."

I had feelings of helplessness. I hated not being able to take away the pain and experiences that hurt my children before they came into the home. There was the fear of doing something wrong to make things worse. I walked on eggshells to avoid triggering their past experiences. The rage, the physical acting out, previous sexual exposure, the projecting of fear on siblings, lack of trust, food hoarding, stealing, and hateful words all came from the place of their pain and trauma. It hit us straight in the gut.

There was also the stress of trying to mesh two sibling groups into one big happy family. It did not exactly happen that way. This has always been a huge stress point for our family.

This depression was hidden to most people. I was a really great faker. I could smile, joke, and pretend like the best of them. I dressed the kids in their best and we stepped out the house as if life was grand. We knew it would continue to be a war zone if we did not make some changes. In my book, *Let Go!*, I discuss how my lifelong issue with food addiction quadrupled and my weight hit an all-time high. Why? I had not allowed God to help me handle the stress. I kept it all inside and ate about everything. I said that right...I didn't pray about it, I ate about it. This caused even more emotional and physical stress, and sickness as I tipped the scale. Being exposed to and feeling the stress of another person's trauma can have ill effects on everyone in the environment. This is why support and self-care are so important.

There were also triggers from my childhood that reared their ugly heads in response to my kids' trauma. One of these very sensitive topics was the sexual abuse I suffered. Helping my children through such challenges triggered something in me that I thought I had dealt with and healed long ago. It was so close and so painful, it literally made me sick to my stomach to revisit. I found myself also dealing with an anger that I had never considered a problem until I became a parent. Where was this coming from? Why was I so angry? It took a while to unpack all the reasons why. It was traced back to a long period of time in my adult life where I felt under the control of a person and organization. I could not express my anger for fear of retribution. This anger, completely unrelated to my children, came out toward them. I had a lot of work to do so that I could be the mom my kids needed me to be for them. I suggest that parents seek therapy if they feel they have unresolved issues that are impeding the relationships that are important to them.

Mom Issues

I must admit that I have mom issues of my own. In my book, *Let Go!*, I discuss my childhood growing up with a mother who struggled with mental illness her entire life. It was tough. It fueled my desire to be a completely different kind of mother. This was not easy.

I found myself time and time again on the receiving end of my children's rage and behavior. It was painful and confusing as I tried to navigate the relationship. I was constantly blaming myself and looking for answers to foster that connection with my kids. It was more challenging with some kids than others. Their rage and behavior rarely focused on their dad.

It was not until I was able to sit down and discuss this concern with my children's therapist and other foster and adoptive moms, that I got it. The therapist's words stung like a bee, yet they brought so much clarity to what I was experiencing. "What you are experiencing is textbook mom issues. You are present to receive the abuse and rage; however, you are not the focus. When they see you, they see the one that abandoned them. It is too scary to allow you to get close to them for fear that you may also abandon or abuse them."

Tuning in with all of my foster and adoptive mom friends, it became obvious that she was absolutely correct. We are the target. Not because they don't love us, but because they are afraid to. This made things so clear and allowed me to respond to my child with more compassion and understanding, instead of anger and disdain. It is not you. It is what you represent. It takes time to gain their trust and change their view of what a mom can be in their lives.

Marriage

Couples that go into foster care or adoption need to do so with their eyes wide open. They need to be trauma competent and their relationship needs to be rock solid before jumping in with two feet. Just like you don't fix a rocky marriage by getting pregnant, you also cannot fix it by adopting a child that comes with a set of their own challenges.

It is imperative that you are supporters of each other's emotional, mental, and physical needs. One person cannot feel like all of the deep diving trauma work is all their responsibility. This has to be a team effort.

I am so thankful for my husband. He is a wise praying man. He is attentive to my emotional state and stress levels. He insists that I take time away when I get overwhelmed. Our thresholds for stress are completely different. We complement each other in so many ways. It is the only way we have been able to help our children heal and thrive without completely losing it. Being on the same page and having a bond that cannot be broken will keep you steady on rough days. Praying together and discussing ideas in handling parenting issues can keep you on one accord.

*"Burnout and caregiver fatigue are contagious
syndromes. Choose your support wisely."*
Eileen Devine, LCSW

There are many times that our children, as many children
do, have tried to divide us on issues that were very
serious. If we were not operating as a unit, it could have
torn us apart. The best gift you can give your children
who have experienced unstable environments is a stable,
strong, and unified marriage. Get out of the house
together without the kids as often as you can. Remember
where this all began and keep that bond strong. No life
experience will be able to break you when you stand
together with the Lord.

If you are not married, it is important that you assemble a
good support system around you. You cannot do this
alone!

Support

It is important that you choose support from the right
people. Those that support your choice to foster or adopt
are important. You do not need whispers of fear and
doubt when you are confident that this is what God has
led you to do. What should my support network look
like? Family, friends, local organizations, your agency,
and possibly your church can be helpful.

Support can come in the form of friendship when you just
need to talk. It can come in the form of training for
trauma care and parenting. There are also church support
groups for foster and adoptive families, some of which

do not require you to be a church member to attend. You may need assistance in the form of respite care by others that understand the unique needs of your kids.

Over the years, I have been a part of a few adoption support groups. I was a part of one group that was nothing more than a festival of complaints. There was no training, no real support, prayer, or even a positive spin. That lasted a very short time. I am not in the business of sharing my children's history and challenges with complete strangers or people who are not close and trusted friends.

I was also part of a support group connected to a church we used to attend. The families in that group are still dear friends of mine today. We were able to share our hearts, pray together, offer encouragement, and share resources and fellowship together. That was a support group. One of those dear friends from that group who understands our babies perfectly offered to take them for a weekend for us to fly to Amelia Island, Florida and renew our vows for our 20th wedding anniversary. It was just the renewal we needed spiritually and as a couple.

Self-Care

Like many moms, I used to think that doing things for myself was selfish. It was difficult rationalizing money or time for something that only benefited me. I suffered in silence, trying to pour from an empty cup. I am so thankful for my husband, who has always pushed me out the door and made me take time for myself. I will be honest: many of those days, I would sit in my car and search the internet for ways to help my kids, buy something for my kids online, or actually in a store filling a cart of things for them.

"You cannot lead a child to a place of healing if you do not know the way yourself."
Dr. Karyn Purvis

The unfortunate thing is that I would complain about my lack of time and peace. I had to question whether it was the pressure being put on me by my family, or by myself. The hard answer was that it was all me. My husband made sure I had the time; I just was not using it for me. So, that is exactly what I started doing. You will be a better mom, dad, or caregiver when you take care of yourself. You can show up for them on the hard days when you have shown up for yourself regularly.

Time alone can mean something different for everyone. I would encourage you to spend time with God daily. However, I am talking about a different kind of self-care. Self-care for me looked like finding a support group for food addiction, giving myself regular pedicures, taking myself to the movies, and reading. It also looks like nature walks, bubble baths, reading a good biography, singing and worshiping uninterrupted, tea with a friend, and trying a new craft or hobby.

I also make sure that I support his interests and give him ample time to do things that he loves. That allows us to be better for each other and our children.

What does self-care look like for you and your spouse? Write it down. You will be a better mom, dad, or caregiver for it. Commit to it NO MATTER WHAT...

Beautiful Moments

It is a beautiful moment when you can have a calm conversation about hard stuff that ends in prayer and hugs instead of slammed doors, yelling, and words we can never take back.

What I Have Learned

I succeed by operating out of my renewed mindset instead of my old way of thinking. This allows me to connect with my kids and maintain that relationship positively.

Prayer

Father, I thank you that your son died not only for my sins, but also for my pain and suffering. He came that I may have life and that I may have it more abundantly. I ask you, Lord, to take this thing that is holding me back from your promises in my life. I give you my fears, anxiety, and pain that cause me to parent and relate to others in a way that does not enrich or restore our relationship. I receive and thank you for total healing.

In Jesus' Name,
Amen

"Healing doesn't mean the trauma never existed. It means the trauma no longer controls our lives."

Unknown

Chapter 4
Is Love Enough?

*A*t the beginning of my journey with foster care and adoption, my perspective was greatly skewed. I knew God wanted me to be a mouthpiece in this area, but I was not quite sure how. I started out volunteering my help to prospective adoptive parents. I even considered turning it into a business. There was a time when I truly believed that everyone should adopt. This was long before I realized the resilience and patience it took to raise a child who had been through so much. Everyone is not ready to say, "NO MATTER WHAT, I am in this for the long haul."

Why isn't love enough? Love in a general sense can have a shallow meaning that is warm and fuzzy. True love is an action word that comes in the form of hard truths, correction, guidance, discipline, and hard work. The feeling alone is not enough. The action that follows that feeling is where the real work is done with our kids who have experienced unimaginable things. As I educated myself, I started listening to adult adoptees and foster alumni to gain an understanding of the real needs of children in their situation. It was a real wake-up call.

A random encounter with an adult adoptee online changed everything for me. They ridiculed my comment and gave me an eye-opening experience as far as my perspective and thinking. What was I doing? I found myself on the wrong side of the fence. What was God trying to tell me?

He was speaking very clearly that the child was the most important person in the adoption equation. It brings the quote by Joyce Maguire Pavao to mind, "Adoption is not about finding children for families, it is about finding families for children." This is not to say that the parents are not important. It is to say that the children should be the focus, not the system or what all the adults in charge want, but what is best for this child.

Armed with new perspective and God's guidance, I completely changed my direction, and everything began to change for me. That is when my career in this area actually started as a child advocate, trauma informed trainer, speaker, and writer. I have continued on that path from that point on. I am doing exactly what God has called me to do.

"I am a huge proponent of family preservation. How can we keep families together in the first place?"

Is foster care or adoption for everyone? NO! A resounding NO! I used to think it was. Many Christians will point out scriptures that admonish us to care for widows and orphans. Do I believe this is God's heart? Yes. Some scriptures such as James 1:27 have been used to guilt many Christians into thinking that everyone should be doing this. If you read the ENTIRE chapter, you will see that it is encouraging people to give their lives for something. Caring for widows and orphans was used as an example of those that are special to God, but certainly not as a mandate for everyone to adopt. To care and advocate, yes.

There are people who are called to help in other ways such as prison ministry, women's ministry, the grieving, the addicted. Most of all, the Great Commission is a call He has required of all of us as believers.

The over-romanticizing of adoption has been a problem. I have been in Christian circles where you feel alienated if this is not part of the vision for your family. Some churches make it their main focus and in turn alienate families who do not feel it is their call to adopt. Much of this comes from a Westernized savior complex that is ingrained into our minds without even recognizing it.

Why is it a problem? I used to ask myself this question often. That was until I began to see foster children moved from home after home with no regard for their need for attachment and permanency. I saw children adopted from other countries and brought home after long charity events thrown to pay for their adoption. Soon they were abandoned and re-homed because it was just too hard. Failed adoptions and multiple foster care placements happen too often. That is what made me rethink my stance on whether or not everyone should adopt. Everyone is not equipped or ready to handle the trauma and behavior of kids who have been through hell and back in their short lives. After the honeymoon period and things start getting hard and unbearable, their new forever family turns their back on them, just like everyone else did in their lives. I am not in the business of convincing people to adopt. That is a conclusion that one has to come to on their own.

Is love enough? I heard this a lot while we were going through our process to adopt from foster care. It was a cliché that you agree with, but you don't really unpack the meaning until you are in the midst of challenges. No. Love is not enough.

We had friends of ours that adopted shortly after we did. He was a precious little boy. He brought with him a series of challenges that they were not prepared for. They prayed and completely acted like his old life was not necessary to acknowledge or unpack. "Just look forward. Look how wonderful your life is now. Why look backwards?" was their stance.

> "I am not in the business of convincing people to adopt. That is a conclusion that one has to come to on their own."

It was not until a few years later that they reached out to me for help and admitted that their approach was unfair and damaging. Love is not enough. Prayer is great; however, your children need some practical application of trauma competency on the part of the parents. A child cannot move forward without settling, understanding, and healing from the past. No matter how amazing the life is that you are providing for your child, it is not enough. **Healing backwards helps them move forward.**

It takes much more than love to compassionately parent a traumatized child. You need to be equipped with tools and knowledge. You need to understand how their past is affecting the present. Most importantly, you must be committed NO MATTER WHAT…

I have seen children with behaviors that disrupted an entire household. This has been true in our home in some instances. We had to be ready for that and know how to create a new normal for everyone to thrive. Every child's response to their past shows up differently. This could lead to out-of-home placement for some children who need extensive help. Make no mistake, their parents need to still be their parents and give them all the support they need to heal and grow into the adult God created them to be.

This is where I come in as a consultant. I no longer wave the "everyone adopt" banner. My role is to step in for training after a family has already determined that this is what they want to do, and when they need support and training.

What if you have a heart for orphans or children in foster care but you do not believe adoption is for your family? There are lots of things you can do. You can volunteer to cook for a foster or adoptive family during those first few days of transition. When we adopted both sibling groups, we had a network of friends that blessed us greatly with meals. It allowed us to transition smoothly without worrying about meal planning in the midst of the chaos. You can also volunteer to babysit or give foster and adoptive parents a respite. Living in an environment where there are several kids healing from trauma can be exhausting and stressful. Offer to spend time with the kids to give the parents a break.

If you are a teacher or work with children or youth in any way, educate yourself. You will be much better at your job if you understand the root of the behaviors you are seeing. Compassion will take the place of ridicule rather quickly.

I am a huge proponent of family preservation. How can we keep families together in the first place? Volunteer for organizations or sponsor families through a reputable organization that focuses on family preservation.

Donate and support organizations that are making a huge difference in the lives of children and families around the world. Most organizations who have proven fruit have all of their financial information available to the public.

It is important to know that there are many ways for believers to get involved and be a blessing to children who do not have a voice. Pray and ask God what he would have you do. Is adoption His plan for your family? If not, then what is?

Beautiful Moments

The most beautiful moments are when a child comes out on the other side of trauma healed and restored.

What I Have Learned

I have learned that everyone is not called to adopt or foster children. If parents are not equipped, they should not do it.

Prayer

Father, please direct and guide me in this decision to foster or adopt children. Let me know if this is your will for our family. Give me the grace and knowledge if it is your will so that I can be an effective healing agent in their lives.

In Jesus' Name,
Amen

"Our children were harmed in relationships and they will experience healing through nurturing relationships."

Dr. Karyn Purvis

Chapter 5
Agent of Healing

*T*he word trauma is an old word; however, it has been all the buzz lately with new research and knowledge regarding its effect and impact on our lives.

Trauma competency is the understanding of the effects of trauma and adverse life experiences on the brain, behavior, and body. A trauma competent parent is not just a parent who understands this, but one who is also able to effectively dissect a behavior and understand the roots and challenges that lead to such behavior.

Studies have shown that the brain of a nurtured and well-cared-for toddler are significantly larger than that of a child who has been neglected, abused, or malnourished. The activity of the brain gives us quite an obvious display of the aftermath that comes from these experiences.

We owe it to ourselves and our children to identify the ways that trauma presents itself in our own lives and make the changes to correct that. It is important to note that the response to trauma can show up differently depending on the person. Commonly we see what appear to be negative behaviors, choices, anger, depression, and lifestyles attached to traumatic childhood experiences. Trauma can also present itself in a vastly different form.

Consider this...

"Childhood trauma can manifest as...The overachiever that is super ambitious and always accomplishing it all, but can never acknowledge their own progress. It can look like the people pleaser that says yes to everything in fear of making others upset. Maybe the strong one that doesn't cry or express emotion and keeps their problems to themselves. Sometimes it is the perfect child who sets extreme standards for their physical body and outward appearance in order to keep up a mask. It may also look like the caretaker who sets out to help everyone around them, but ends up self-abandoning."
~unknown author~

When adopting one of my children, I was told that they would always be emotionally delayed. I had understood physical delays, and I even understood cognitive delays. I found it hard to understand how an emotional delay displayed itself. It only took a few years to recognize exactly what that meant. My child was growing physically, academically, and otherwise. However, they were emotionally behind their peers in how they related to people and handled complex circumstances.

Many children who have experienced early trauma would show multiple signs of delay. It is an unrealistic expectation of an eleven-year-old who has been neglected and abused to perform, act, and display the age-appropriate actions of a nurtured and well-cared-for eleven-year-old. This may not be the case across the board in all of the child's development. As I mentioned above, my child seemed right on point with all other milestones.

These traumatic experiences can adversely affect a person long term. Trauma competent parents can reduce the impact of that and its long-term effects by being knowledgeable and developing systems, boundaries, and a nurturing environment for a child to thrive in. With help and encouragement, children can become victorious over the circumstances that dominated their early lives.

"A trauma competent parent is not just a parent who understands trauma, but one who is also able to effectively dissect a behavior and understand the roots and challenges that lead to such behavior."

One way that we have approached healing is through prayer and compassion. I try to share the truth of the state of their biological family's lives and all of the circumstances that led up to their own trauma. Without excusing the behavior, abuse, and pain that they endured, we try to develop a sense of compassion for their families by praying together for them, recognizing that the parents themselves were the product of adverse traumatic events. This was a light bulb moment for a few of my kids.

One day I decided to address my very own childhood trauma. It was a turning point in my parenting. I recognized my own challenges due to the trauma I had suffered. This gave me a better view of the fears, behavior, and needs of my children as a result of their trauma. It gave me perspective and compassion for them on a new level. It was a beautiful moment. I have learned that it is one thing to understand trauma and its effects. It is an entirely different thing to operate as a trauma competent care giver and walk this thing out.

Trauma Competent Parenting is…

➤ Counter intuitive – it is oftentimes the opposite of what many think should be done in a normal situation.

➤ A response instead of a reaction – it is a well thought out response taking into account the root of the behavior or fear the child is challenged with.

➤ Not the same as traditional parenting – it is a different way of thinking and looking at the triggers of our children.

➤ Hard work – it takes practice, repetition, and time to know what works best for each child and their differing experiences.

➤ Creativity – it is trying things until you find a connection that brings peace and growth for everyone involved.

➤ Grace – it is parenting our children in the way that God parents us. It does not shame or punish. Showing love and support even when we stumble; understanding our challenges.

Becoming an Agent of Healing

It is so important for us to know what our children have endured before they step foot into our home. Our children need an agent of healing that is committed to walking them through the hard feelings, behaviors, and triggers left from the aftermath of days gone by. Asking as many questions as possible of the agency and reading every page in their file is crucial to be able to help them.

Yes, it matters! The day that we decided to adopt our younger three children, before even meeting them, the agency sent over the files. I read through them thoroughly, only to come to a full stop two years prior to the current date. My agency had just received their file from another state agency. There were no pictures of my children. The files were missing two years of their lives. I was furious! The children were six, five, and three years old. What happened to them for those two years in foster care? Where were they? Who were they with? What were their experiences? Good, traumatic, scary…I would never know.

> *"Imagine a world where every child's cry is*
> *met by loving adults."*
> Dr. Karyn Purvis

We went into this determined to parent them compassionately and give them an environment in which they could heal and thrive. Missing that information was very difficult in determining how to approach certain things.

For example, one child was terrified of showers. How was I supposed to understand that the first time that I attempted to have him take a shower? Thankfully one of the other children remembered enough to understand why he was so afraid based on punishments he received in one of his foster homes.

These are situations that cause us to re-traumatize children by ignorance. Knowing what they have been through to the best of your ability is crucial to developing trust and attachment with the child.

This scenario has played out in our home so many times, where Dad and I had to decode past trauma experiences in order to not re-offend and bring more pain to a situation.

In order to become an agent of healing, you must become a student of your children. Observing, praying, and asking questions helps you develop that bond and safe place for them.

> ## "We must do our part, and allow God to do His!"

I have seen time and time again, parents walk their child into a therapist's office and say, "Fix them!" Healing is a process and it takes everyone involved to help the child get there. Believe it or not, the parent and their perspective is a major determining factor in the process of restoration in a child's life.

Parents need to change their perspective and behavior just as much, if not more, than the child. Many times, it is our response to their trauma and behavior that is setting an atmosphere that perpetuates our children's lack of trust and continual fear.

I am reminded of a series of therapy appointments that I went to with one of my children. The therapist was asking me a lot of questions about myself, my own trauma, and experiences. After a while, I got irritated. *We are here to deal with my child's behavior*, I thought to myself. Boy, was I wrong. My attitude, perspective, my own trauma, and response to my children have EVERYTHING to do with how effective therapy will be and whether my child will experience the healing they desperately need. It was a serious light bulb moment for me. I was just as important in the equation of my child's healing and behavior as my child. Mind blown!

"Love alone is NOT enough and time does NOT heal all wounds!"

Therapists often tell you when a child starts therapy to expect things to get stirred up before they settle. It is not easy digging through old things without revisiting the experiences and emotions attached to those memories.

Sometimes that looks like rebellion, misbehavior, and anger in a child. We have to prepare ourselves to respond with compassion while we are rehashing and working toward healing for our children.

God has a master plan for you and for the children that you are caring for. When you seek Him for help, provision and guidance, His word says that you will find Him, when you seek with your whole heart. God knows your desire to care for and nurture these children. He loves them even more than you do. This is a partnership! God has a plan and you are part of it. The pain that children have suffered due to trauma does not just go away. It does not disappear because they now have a family.

As much as we want to FIX all the things that have gone wrong in their lives and make it all right, we do not have the power to do that. We do have God's wisdom and the ability to be agents of healing.

What does that mean?
An agent is a representative of a greater power. The agent cannot heal themselves, but they can be used by God to facilitate that healing.

How?
Providing an environment that facilitates peace, a listening ear, safety, and love. By meeting all physical, emotional, and spiritual needs.

We must do our part and allow God to do His! You can rest in the fact that when you are at the end of yourself and your children are suffering from their past, He is there. He hears your cries, your prayers, and is ready to meet you and your family right where you are. Trust Him NO MATTER WHAT...

Beautiful Moments

After a year of being with our family, her sixth home, one of my daughters asked me to put her suitcase in the basement. She had slept with it next to her bedroom door for that entire year, just in case. It was a precious moment when she decided to trust that this time was different and that this was home.

What I Have Learned

I learned that my response to my children's trauma is just as important as their own response. I needed to change and grow just as much as they did in order to become an agent of healing for them.

Prayer

God, help me to see who my children are. Help me to see them through your eyes and compassion. Give me insight, dear Lord, into the pain that they have suffered at the hands of others. Give me wisdom, unconditional love, and direction in parenting their unique needs. Father, let me be an agent of healing in the lives of the beautiful children you have placed in my care.

In Jesus' Name,
Amen

"It was more empowering for my kids to be mad than to be sad. It was especially easier to be mad than to be vulnerable and feel powerless. It's amazing how kids push us away, when they really want us to hold them close."

Tricia Goyer
Calming Angry Kids

Chapter 6
A Child's Perspective

*A*doption is a complex thing. While exciting and the beginning of something brand new, it is also the end of something else. No adoption happens without loss. When we brought our first two children home, we had no idea or concept of the depth of loss that takes place in adoption. We desperately wanted to be parents and when we got that phone call, the world stopped. It was finally happening: after several miscarriages and years of trying, we were finally going to be parents. So, needless to say, we shouted it from the roof tops and bought out the stores preparing for our little ones. They were two and three years old at the time.

> *"While we are blowing up balloons and throwing epic parties, a child may still be grieving and may not know how to respond to your happiness during a time when they do not know how to feel."*

We had two showers that were totally over the top. My husband's job had thrown a company-wide party and the employees showered us with so many gifts, gift cards, stuffed animals, and clothes, it was amazing. The other shower was thrown by our closest friends from our church. Lots of people showed up that day and it was awesome, until it was time for our little ones to arrive with their foster parents. Not realizing it, we had not had "the talk" with the little ones on their level as far as what was going to transpire. Their foster parents were the only parents they had ever known, so this party that was supposed to be for them was completely odd. Was it a birthday party, Christmas, or what? We began to see their stress level rise significantly when everyone wanted to tour the house and see the gorgeous rooms we decorated for our new little ones and their decked-out playroom. They had no idea why they had a room at my house.

I realized after that day that we had gone about this thing all wrong. It was okay to be excited, but we skipped a few steps in between. We never had the necessary conversations. We did not give them a chance to get to know their new environment and us before parading them before the world. If I could do it all over again, I would!

We have since adopted four more children, a sibling of the first two kids, and another sibling set of three in 2013. We now have six kids. This time we did things differently. We took it slow. We paid close attention to their emotional cues and followed their lead. We did not throw a shindig of epic proportion this time. Instead we made it intimate, family focused, and waited a bit after placement to give everyone time to mesh as a family of eight.

Am I saying that I am against the fanfare for newly adopted children? No, not at all. I am saying that following the child's lead is important, and being totally upfront about what is happening in their life is key. It may not affect an infant as much. However, when you have an older child who is being separated indefinitely from their first family, it is bittersweet. While we are blowing up balloons and throwing epic parties, a child may still be grieving. They may not know how to respond to your happiness during a time when they do not know how to feel. You are asking them to be excited at the same time they are hurting because they may never see their family again.

Get excited! Celebrate the occasion, but always remember their little hearts and what they may be going through during that time. Give them time to process the changes in their lives and the transition will be much smoother. Do what is best for your child NO MATTER WHAT...

Beautiful Moments

With both sibling groups, the most precious moments during their transitions into our family were when the crowds were gone and the parties were over. We were alone together to establish ourselves as a family.

What I Have Learned

Personal growth is beautiful. They say when you know better, do better. Shifting my perspective from my needs to my children's needs during this transition established a relationship where they can share their feelings without fear.

Prayer

Father, let me see this process of foster care/adoption through the eyes of my child. Give me wisdom to make decisions and provide an environment that will help them feel loved and at home in this new environment. Let there be many opportunities to connect and begin a relationship that will grow stronger by the day.

In Jesus' Name,
Amen

"My words of wisdom to anyone thinking about becoming a foster parent is to go ALL IN. You will never regret the investment of time, love, and compassion you have sown into the life of a child."

Sarah Dumas

Chapter 7
Fostering the Future

*T*he number one goal of foster care is and should always be to reunite the family that has been separated. It was put in place to intervene and assist when issues threaten to break up families. It is important to go into this with the right perspective. Over the decades, the numbers of children in care have risen in the US and less and less children are reunited with their families. This is an unfortunate truth that we face in our country.

When we began this journey, we considered temporary foster care. It was a hard decision to not pursue it. However, the heartache that we had experienced through so much pain already made us rethink if we could handle further emotional loss.

"The number one goal of foster care is and should always be to reunite the family that has been separated."

That is when we decided to do foster-to-adopt. We wanted to consider children who had been waiting a long time and were hard to place. These cases generally lead to adoption because they have been in the system longer than any child should ever be. Both sibling groups we adopted were waiting for a family and were considered hard to place because of the size of the sibling group, ages, race, and challenges.

You may have decided that foster care is your calling and that adoption is not. The ability to love a child for however long they are in your care, and making them feel safe and valued, is a gift. I believe it takes a very special person to foster and advocate for a child's reunification with their family.

Foster Care Globally

Although my husband and I adopted through foster care in the United States, family-based care is becoming a movement throughout the world, replacing institutional care. Some countries are further along in developing a family-based care model than others. The eradication of institutional living for children is the goal across the globe. In the US, the goal is reunification first. If that is not possible, the goal is permanence.

In many countries where I have trained foster parents and social workers, reunification is the first goal as well. However, many of the countries use foster care as a model of permanence for children, not allowing them to be legally adopted by another family. Sometimes laws do not permit this, but the families that care for them make a lifetime commitment to the children.

Like any other goal you set out to pursue, doing it well should be your number one priority. There are several areas in which you need to focus to do this, and do it with the ultimate impact on the lives of the children that come into your home. Foster care is not just a holding place. It is not simply for shelter, food, and safety. It can and should be so much more.

Excellence

Do you think that any company starts with the goal to be average? I don't think any of us ever start a job or undertake a major project with the intention of failing. Just like other endeavors, being a foster parent deserves your utmost effort and heart. You are handling precious lives. Approach this with the highest level of excellence as if someone's life depends on it, because it does.

Organize Your Home

Any job you have ever had has required you to get organized and have a system to complete that job efficiently. Getting organized can make your experience much smoother. Just like you would if you were having a new baby, you may have to do some organizing to make sure the house is ready for someone else. Is your house logistically ready to foster? Make a list of everything you may need. Collect an array of supplies for the age group that you are open to. Clothes, bedding, toys, snacks, car seats, and other things. If you keep these things on hand, you will always be ready for a placement.

Organize Your Records/Pictures

Keep a filing system for each child that is and has been in your home. This allows you insight into their experiences and helps you relate to them. Keep a journal of a child's time in your home for their files and for them to take with them. This gives them a memory of that time in their life. Take as many pictures as you can of the kids in your care; hard copies can be put in an album for them to take with them when they return home or move on. Do not post pictures on social media of children who are in foster care; this is generally against the rules for most agencies.

Receiving a New Placement

Have a system to receive each new placement. If you are in a frenzy, the child will definitely feel the anxiety. They are already in a state of turmoil, so being organized can bring calm to this transition. Create a new placement checklist that includes practical things to do, questions to ask the agency, and a list of warm fuzzies. What do I mean by warm fuzzies? What things can you do to make this transition easier for the child? Make cookies, find out their favorite meal, cancel the family plans, and anything else you can do to welcome them with open arms into a calm and prepared environment.

"The ability to love a child for however long they are in your care, and making them feel safe and valued, is a gift."

Reunification with Parents or Adoption

What will be your process when a child is reuniting or being adopted by another family? How can you make this process a smooth and loving move for them? Maybe it is hosting a dinner at your home for their family or the new adoptive family or possibly a gift from your family that they can cherish and take with them, like a photo album, their favorite treats, a favorite book, or pajamas. The goal is to be instrumental in this transition into the next phase of their life.

Advocacy

Who's on their side? Talk to your kids. Find out their "love language" and what makes them feel supported.

In what areas do they need the most advocacy? That answer may be different for each child. That child needs to know that YOU will have their back. You have to be ready to fight for the services they need. Children cannot fight for themselves in all of these areas. The last thing we want to do is add to the trauma they have already experienced. Be fluent and familiar with all the information regarding each child's history to better serve them.

Possible Advocacy Needs
- Physical/Occupational Therapy
- IEPs
- Counseling
- Medication
- Medical Intervention
- Insurance

Healing
With six different kids, we had to be students of their individual needs. We have kids with very logical fears and some very illogical fears that stem from their past trauma. We had to familiarize ourselves with what made them feel safe and secure, whether it made sense to us or not.

How can you help them begin healing?
- Ownership of their body
- Providing a sense of safety
- Taking their fears seriously

Inclusion, not Exclusion

They should not feel like the black sheep because they are in foster care. They should have the same privileges as anyone else in the family unless they have proven to be untrustworthy in an area. Even then, they need the opportunity to regain trust.

"The last thing we want to do is add to the trauma they have already experienced."

Preparation

Your home is a place of preparation for the next stage of their lives. What is **your role** in their life? How can you prepare them?

- Foster - If you are simply fostering and not adopting, your role is healing, parenting, support, safety, and stability while in your care. No matter how long. When a child looks back, they need to remember their time with you as safe, pleasant, and loving!

- Reunification - Visitations, healing, safety, support, and preparation to return home. How can you help make reunification with their family smooth and comfortable?

- Pre-Adopt - Healing, parenting, and transition into life as a permanent member of the family as soon as placement takes place with all rights and privileges of other family members. What is your plan to make the transition smooth and welcoming?

- Emergency/Respite/Safe Family - Safety, support, and preparation for the next step in their life. Establish a connection that will be with them long after they are gone.

I would like to share with you a few experiences I have had with three different foster moms in our journey toward foster adoption. They were polar opposites in personality and how they viewed their role in our children's lives. I think each of them had positive qualities that make for a great foster parent, and other qualities that could affect the esteem of children for years to come.

Foster Mom 1
Positive: dogmatic advocate, loving, prepared, extremely organized

Negative: controlling, could not let go, skeptical

Foster Mom 2
Positive: loving, well informed, organized, passionate

Negative: health impeded her ability to be hands on with small children

Foster Mom 3
Positive: children's physical needs were met

Negative: disconnected, mean, uninterested, irritated, and unwilling to be helpful, treated them like she wanted them to leave

Don'ts

- Don't blame them for their life's circumstances.
- Don't make them feel like second-class kids who don't deserve happiness or nice things.
- Don't disconnect emotionally…even when their behavior is difficult to handle.
- Don't speak words that hurt.
- Don't be lazy.
- Don't move their belongings in trash bags.

Do's

- Love them if only for 1 day, 1 week, or 1 month.
- Let them know that they matter to you and others.
- Give them words of encouragement for their future.
- Esteem them.
- Keep their story to yourself.
- Find out how to do their hair…it is very important.
- Love them, love them, love them.
- Take lots of pictures no matter how long they are with you…they need this!
- Make an effort to work well with others during transitions (parents, social workers, CASA, teachers, etc.).

Beautiful Moments

It was a beautiful moment when I was able to reunite one of my sons with his foster mother who adored him. For her to see him blossom from a sickly newborn into a brilliant and handsome young man was a gift to her, my son, and ourselves as parents.

What I Have Learned

I learned that the hearts of the foster parents who walked with my kids through the beginnings of a very scary journey need compassion and care. They do hard work with love and patience.

Prayer

Father, I pray for foster families in my church and community. Bless them for their willingness to support family reunification and love on children during such a difficult time. Lord, let me know if the foster care ministry is for our family. Give us the strength and wisdom to walk this road well. If not, allow me to be a blessing to those who do.

In Jesus' Name,
Amen

"Every child has NOT had the benefit of nurturing, comfort, and connection in infancy and childhood. We have to understand the profound difference this makes."

Post Institute

Chapter 8
Smooth Transitions

*I*n 2005, when we completed our application for adoption, home study, and interviews, we really were not prepared for our life to change all that much. We were ministers in a large church. This church was a seven-day-a-week church, meaning that there was something going on every day of the week. Between my husband and myself, we were either in charge of or a part of several departments. This included meetings, teaching classes, rehearsals, and preparations for huge events. Not sure what we thought would change when we became parents, but we were definitely in for a wake-up call.

In 2006, when we finally took placement of two amazing little kids, we were ready to take on the world. We continued on our journey as ministers and dragged them along for the ride. All the meetings, rehearsals, event preparation, training, and four church services a week kept us running like crazy. No one ever told us to slow down, take time off, or adjust our lives. Out of commitment and loyalty, we continued as long as we could, until we couldn't.

Once my children's little brother was born and joined the family as well, things came to a halt. He was on a heart monitor and had a few health issues that caused concern. I tried to keep up. I really did. I tried to remain committed and engaged in all the areas that I was responsible for. It literally became too much for me to handle. I then began lagging, quitting, and developed quite a bitter stance about the church. I was hurt that I was expected to be super woman. In less than a nine-month period, I had adopted two toddlers and a newborn. No one cared that my personal life changed, only that I was reliable and present when they needed me. I failed to ask for help or grace. Instead I quit many things altogether.

I later resigned from my job after trying to juggle a full-time career in human resources, ministerial duties, marriage, and my newest role as a mom of three small children. Being home with my children was just the ticket to normalizing our transition and bonding experience. Many times, I wish I would have stayed home from the very beginning to nurture a deeper bond with our two oldest children. Since 2007, I have been home and I would not have it any other way.

"Not sure what we thought would change when we became parents, but we were definitely in for a wake-up call."

What my children needed in those first months after placement was stability and calm. Our life was anything but that. They were just added to the chaos and busyness, which did not allow for a lot of time for bonding and connection.

Seven years later when we brought our youngest three children home, we were determined not to repeat the same mistakes. We prepared the home, our lifestyle, and schedules to accommodate as much family time as possible. Our goal was a calm and quiet transition.

Slow Down

This is why I stress to new foster and adoptive parents to expect their life to change. Plan for the transition to be as smooth as possible. Whatever changes you can make leading up to placement, make them.

Take time off work, if possible. By law, companies consider adoption to fall under the FMLA (Family Medical Leave Act) benefit. This will allow for you to focus solely on making this a better transition.

Lighten your schedule from outside commitments such as church, organizations, volunteer positions, and school-related activities or studies. Create spaces of time for social worker visits, therapy and doctor appointments, biological family visits (if applicable), and one-on-one time with you. Canceling family plans may be in order in some situations. Every new placement needs time to adjust before being thrust into a world of new routines and relationships.

Try to explain in advance to family and friends that you will need a moment to establish yourselves in the child's life as their parents. It is best to do this before you introduce a multitude of people into their lives. Help them to understand how trauma and connection work as to limit offense.

Logistics

Prepare your home for another family member the same way you would a newborn. The child should have ample space to grow and thrive. Think through the logistics of living in advance, such as adding more space at the table, more room in the playroom for a new child, drawer and closet space, and storage. Another important thing to consider is transportation. Each time we adopted our sibling groups, we had to purchase a new vehicle that would fit our growing family.

When preparing for our newest arrivals, I completely reconfigured the sleeping arrangements. The fun of decorating kids' rooms has always excited me. The girls' room was a royal pink palace surrounded by all things girly. It literally looked like something out of a magazine. The two older boys had a room with a sports theme. The two younger boys' room was decorated in a Spider-Man theme, which was a favorite at the time.

"Plan for the transition to be as smooth as possible. Whatever changes you can make leading up to placement, make them."

Finances

Even if you have foster care or adoption subsidy from your state, it is certainly not the amount it takes to properly care for a child. Consider what the increased cost will look like for your new addition. Will they be in childcare or private school? Boy oh boy, was I blindsided by the cost of having an infant and two toddlers in daycare all at once. This was a huge expense. What about that new car, or more groceries, formula, diapers, clothes? These things add up.

When you are bringing a new child home, you want your focus to be on bonding, not financial stress. That is why it is important to count up the cost beforehand so that you can prepare and have fewer financial surprises.

Environment

I am big on environment, and how the atmosphere in my home affects our family. How can you adjust the environment in your home to be inviting and calming for a child who has already been through so much? What do I mean by the environment? I mean the five senses.

Sound – Are there sounds that bring peace and calm in the home?

Sight – Is the home clean, orderly, and set up in an inviting way that brings peace and comfort?

Smell – Are there candles, fresh sheets, favorite meals, fresh air, and pleasant aromas flowing throughout the home?

Touch – Are there places of comfort to relax that create joy and pleasant memories?

Taste – Are there yummy and healthy meals being prepared with care for those who call this home?

International Adoption & Transracial Adoption

There is so much to consider when bringing new children into your home. When you adopt internationally or a child of a different race, there are even more things to keep in mind. Not only is your child suffering from the loss of their biological family and home, they are also suffering other losses such as culture, language, foods, smells, friends, and the comforts of familiarity.

Although our children resemble me and their dad, they are a beautiful and multi-cultural mix themselves. All of them have an African American heritage in common. However, they all share Mexican heritage on their biological maternal side. One of my daughters is also half Haitian. We don't just want to honor their African American heritage, but their Mexican and Haitian heritage as well.

It is important to be very sensitive to their need to adjust and become comfortable in their new environment and culture. It is new, scary, and different. There are several ways to bring some of those familiar elements into your home. A few years ago, I taught a class to a group of parents who have adopted children outside of their race. It was called Honoring Your Children's Culture and Heritage. Here are a few of the things that we discussed that are very important to children who are entering unfamiliar surroundings.

- When traveling to their country of birth (if applicable), be sure to purchase or collect significant items that represent their culture.

- Try to find cuisine in your city that is from the same region/culture as your child. Even try to recreate recipes with your child that remind them of home.

- Familiar music is always soothing to a child yearning for home.

- Learn how to manage their skin and hair properly, as this is important to your child's confidence and cultural identity.

- Find multi-cultural events, activities, schools, and sports in your community, or nearby, for your child to be a part of. Children need to see themselves represented in others in their community. It is worth the effort to step outside of your comfort zone.

- Respect what makes them uncomfortable, and make others respect their boundaries and history.

Adding to the Family

Whether you are adding to your family of biological kids or children that were previously adopted, it is a huge transition. There are many ways that you can make this transition smoother. Be advised that any time you are dealing with children, there will be hiccups and hard days. The transition will most likely not be perfect, but you can help make it better for all involved.

 The children who are already in the home need to know that they are still loved, valued, and not being replaced. It will be important to spend one-on-one time with each child to listen and respond to any worries, concerns, or excitement that they have regarding the new addition. We spent a lot of time with our oldest kids explaining some of the changes that would happen. Their focus was on having more kids to play with. We had to help them understand that they were new "friends" that would never leave. It was just pure excitement for them.

I, however, was an emotional mess. I knew they did not get the gravity of what was about to happen multiplied by three. My oldest was always the only girl, and she relished in her "Daddy's little girl" position. Our oldest son was a child who did not ask for much attention, but he needed it desperately. How was I gonna make sure he did not get lost among the crowd of squeaky wheels? My youngest son at the time had been the baby attached at my hip for the first seven years of his life. How would he transition from being the baby to being trumped three times by the new children? We knew that what we were doing was what God wanted, but that did not make the concerns any less frightening for me.

If the children in your home are old enough to understand foster care, orphanage life, and the trauma connected to that, explain. They need to know, without too much detail, that the new addition to your family may have fears, feelings, and experiences that they don't understand. This is where modeling compassion comes in.

"We knew that what we were doing was what God wanted, but that did not make the concerns any less frightening for me."

When changing the logistics and systems of operation in your home, enlist your children to help. It is easier to make them a part of it. Seeing all the changes and feeling like the new child is taking something away from them, their space, and their routine can cause an uproar. Speaking of routine, while freeing up space to prepare for this transition, try to keep your current children in a routine that does not upset their comfort.

During the visitation process with our youngest three children, Dad and I visited with them a few times before we introduced the kids.

The new kids also had to be prepared for the prospect of three older siblings. The oldest had always been the oldest and the only girl as well. She was not fond of the idea of a big sister. The middle child needed more care and focus based on the trauma he had endured in foster care. The baby was oblivious to what was happening. So many decisions had been made in the short three years of his life that did not include his voice. To him, it was just another home. I knew this was going to be tough.

The time came to introduce the sibling groups. I was very nervous and just wanted it all to go smoothly. I was determined to create an atmosphere where their relationship could flourish NO MATTER WHAT...

Visitations went well as the kids played and got to know one another. I knew that things would not always be laughter and fun, but for that moment, it was great. All of the things I have mentioned can make the transition a smooth one. It takes time and effort, but it will set the tone for relationships, peace, and sanity for all involved. Take this transition time seriously.

Beautiful Moments

There is a picture in our living room that represents a beautiful moment that I will always cherish. It is a picture of all six children laying on the floor in a circle and looking up at the camera. I look at it every single day and smile. It was the first day that they all met and became one family.

What I Have Learned

I have learned that I cannot control everything; however, there are some things I can prepare for that will make things easier for everyone. Creating systems and thinking through this transition was helpful for all of us.

Prayer

Father, give me wisdom, resources, and support to make this transition a smooth one. Help me to prepare my family, home, and life for this change. Give us peace as we proceed in adding to our family. Let this be a place of refuge, joy, and growth for us all.

In Jesus' Name,
Amen

"You can recover from all that happened to you!"

Sebern Fisher

Chapter 9
Let's Talk

*T*hree-year-old: "Mom, you said that God gave me to you, right?"

Me: "Yes. Honey, you were a blessing from God."

Three-year-old: "Then where did God get me from?"

Woah! I knew the questions were coming and I would be ready when they did. Only they came years earlier than I expected, and I was NOT ready.

When we brought our first two children home after a two-month long visitation, we were ecstatic to finally be parents. They were two and three years old at the time. We were determined to be honest and upfront about their lives, time in foster care, and adoption from the very beginning. Intentions are good, but when it is time to act, it is easy to get cold feet and say all of the cliché phrases used for adoption over the ages, like:

"You were not born in my tummy, but in my heart."

"You are special, because you were chosen."

"We adopted you just like God adopted us as His children."

There are too many of these avoidance attempts to count flying around foster and adoptive homes. Some are catchy and sweet, some problematic in their concept.

Others are too complicated for a little one to understand. All of them are ways to avoid the hard things, those hard conversations that get at the heart of who your child is, where they came from, and why.

Days of Old

Globally, the way that adoption was handled was cold and brutal. It was not to be mentioned. Secrets loomed in the shadows of families for generations, with the support of governments here and abroad supporting closed records, destroyed files, and archaic laws that left adoptees heartbroken and clueless about themselves and their history.

Imagine with me for a minute, your home, parents, and everything familiar and dear to you, taken in an instant, and NO ONE WILL TELL YOU WHY OR HOW ALL THIS HAPPENED. Imagine cliché phrases thrown at you in code as if to mask this hidden agenda that you are not privy to. What if someone told you that you have a great life now, so why do your old family and life matter? You would fight to the end to get to the bottom of the upset that has become your life. You would expect answers and retribution.

This is what it is like for our children, to be taken away with no power to choose where they go, who they go with, and what happens next. We owe them a soft place to land and conversations that help them understand what is happening and what we are doing to help. If we think this would be an invasive and unfair event in our own lives, think of our children, who have no power and limited ability to understand their own emotions. **Lies destroy families**. We have to do the hard things, no matter how uncomfortable they become.

"Sometimes having hard conversations with your kids will look like you sharing your childhood stories that they can relate to."

Shortly after my son asked me that question, we got a frame and placed a picture on our mantel of the first day that we met. It became a conversation piece for the first couple of years that they were with us. They would point to the picture and talk about what we did on the day we met. They would talk about the toys they played with and the food they ate that day. This was all deliberate. Even though they were very young, we wanted to start with the truth, unlike many generations before us that treated such subjects as taboo. This picture spoke two things to our little ones before they could even articulate what adoption was. One, that they had a life before us. Two, that we were willing to talk about it.

Infant Adoption

Older children are not the only ones affected by the separation from their first family. Research shows that even the chemistry in the baby's brain is altered by this separation. Many adults who were adopted as infants can attest to the longing in their heart for someone they never knew. The worst thing we can do as foster or adoptive parents is to dismiss these feelings because of their age at separation.

Statistics show that private infant adoption is declining in the US. This is partially because of the many organizations that exist to help mothers with resources to parent their children. Other reasons are due to less life-affirming choices.

Another beautiful changing trend in private adoption is that many mothers choose an open adoption. This allows them to develop some level of connection and relationship with their child even though they are being raised by another family. This option keeps truth at the forefront of the child's story.

Talking to Your Kids about Their Story

Your approach to these difficult conversations is critical. Your children should never feel as if their story is something to be ashamed of. Start these conversations early with little ones.

When talking about these topics, I always make sure that my children recognize that the break-up of their family unit was not their fault. Teach your children to externalize their birth family's actions.

Never tell a child that you have adopted that they were destined to be part of your family. That is not true! Telling them this gives them the notion that God desired for them to go through absolute hell before making it to your doorstep. I don't know about you, but I don't serve a God who causes pain, but one that heals the pain caused by this fallen world.

I adore my children and cannot imagine my life without them. However, it is God's desire for every child to grow up with their biological family. When circumstances, bad choices, and the cares of this world get in the way of that, HE has a safety net for his beloved children.

I don't mind being that safety net. As a matter of fact, I am honored to be my children's safety net. However, I will not pretend that this was a predestined plan as if God caused them pain on purpose to get them to me. People caused them pain; we were there to receive them in that aftermath with open arms.

I was working with a family years ago who dealt with a challenging situation when adopting from foster care. The children were not being cared for, fed regularly, or looked after consistently. The older child, who was five years old, was left in charge of an infant. The child was given unreasonable instructions by their mom that they did not obey. As a result of the child not listening, the condition of their home life and lack of parenting was brought to the attention of authorities.

The siblings were soon placed in foster care, later to be joined by more biological siblings that followed. One of the things that their new parents had to help their oldest child with was guilt and shame. She thought she was to blame for their removal. It takes time to deprogram a child who has been told such things by her biological family. Talking through these things and bringing comfort to your child in the process of addressing feelings like this is paramount.

What if I don't know my child's story? Lying or making up cute little stories is not the answer. If you don't know, say you don't know. Be open to your kids' questions. Be as proactive as possible to find out what you can through your agency and the paperwork provided to you.

One practice we have in our home is creating an open and free atmosphere within our four walls. Our kids know that they can ask questions, discuss memories, cry, be angry, and wonder out loud whenever they want. We want our home to be a healing atmosphere where they don't have to pretend and hide their feelings.

As parents, we cannot feel intimidated when our kids want to know more about who they are and the circumstances surrounding their life. They should not feel like they are offending us by sharing their thoughts and feelings about their history and family.

There may be two different stories that you hear from your kids. Fantasy vs Horror. They have to be allowed to see things in multiple ways. Oftentimes their memories can take on both a fantasy and a horror film all in one. Although they may have been neglected or abused in some ways, kids often keep a sense of loyalty to their birth family.

"If you really want your children to respect you, let them speak! Give them safe space to say how they really feel without fear of how your pride will react. It doesn't matter if they are always right or 'good,' it matters that they are allowed to be real with you."
Brooke Hampton

Value their birth connections and positive memories. Never make them feel bad about loving their parents. Allow them to go through whatever phases they need to so they can come to their own conclusions with gentle guidance. It is not a good idea to bad mouth their first family. This may be difficult when you see your child struggling with an issue that is related to the abuse or neglect they suffered.

Sometimes these conversations can be scary and downright uncomfortable for everyone. When talking to your kids, you must push past the fear for your child's mental health and emotional wellness!

"They should not feel like they are offending us by sharing their thoughts and feelings about their history and family."

Many parents are afraid that they won't know what to say, or when to say it. There are many things to consider when starting the conversation. I have found that my children's questions have indicated their readiness and timing of conversations. The more detailed and complicated their curiosity, it will give you clues to dive deeper. Using discretion with undesirable details, you can begin to unfold the timeline of their short lives with compassion. Some of the more graphic details regarding neglect and abuse need to be saved for a later time when they are older and mature enough to handle them.

One of my children was about eleven when we began discussing the origin of some of the things they were struggling with. At that time, they were mature enough to hear some harder truths and develop a resolve within themselves to beat the challenges they were facing. Trauma experts have said that a child should be aware of the complete story of their life by their preteen years. The teen years are too late to reveal such sensitive information when so many other challenges present themselves. This should be a continual conversation from the moment they enter your life into adulthood.

The parents and/or grandparents need to be a united front. Everyone should be on the same page. The parents need to decide what and when information is shared with the child based on their maturity. Sharing with others in the family such as aunts, uncles, siblings, or even grandparents is the parent's role.

All of my children have challenges in different areas as a result of trauma, whether it be in utero, or after birth. However, only one of my children has vivid memories of their life and family before coming to live with us due to her age.

"Lying or making up cute little stories is not the answer. If you don't know, say you don't know."

How do we handle each child based on stage and personality? All of my kids feel differently about their stories and how they talk about them. My oldest child will shout to the rooftops about her foster care and adoption experience. There are times we have to remind her what is and is not shareable information. I have two sons who are very sensitive about their story and would prefer to talk privately about their thoughts and feelings that often have strong emotions. Another daughter is very open to discussing things openly among family but does not like to discuss it with others, or to be singled out because of it. I have two younger sons who were very young when they entered the system. Neither asks questions or talks about anything regarding their first family or experiences. I find myself asking them if they would like to. I do this to ensure they are aware that we are here to talk when they are ready.

Over the years, we have found God-ordained moments here and there to share and plant seeds of hope and healing regarding their lives and families. Many late-night cries, questions, and cuddles have revealed deep hurt and confusion. We don't push or require them to talk, unless we can clearly see that they are harboring something painful that is affecting them in other ways. They are all confident in the fact that they can talk in an uninhibited way with us about their history whenever they desire.

When talking with young children, there are a few things to keep in mind:

- Don't make things complicated.

- Create a bedtime story surrounding the coming together of your family and tell it often. This is something that we did that was helpful during those early years.

- Use books to help them make sense of things.

- Get help. Sometimes a therapist, minister, or trusted and experienced friend can help mediate.

- Have them repeat what you discuss. This helps with clarity in any conversation.

- Take their cues. I can always tell when my kids are done talking. I have learned my lesson by trying to drag on a conversation that was too overwhelming for them. Stop when they stop.

- Express permanence and safety often. Assure them that scary things will not happen here.

- Help them work through bad memories. Pay attention and be present when they are triggered.

- Let them cry/tantrum. When sharing such information, it stirs up lots of emotions. Understand the source and allow them to feel.

When talking to older kids about their story, here are a few tips:

- Be honest. They know more about their story than you do. Ask questions to get an understanding of what took place in their lives.

- Adolescents and teens may require a completely different approach. They may have a very clear view of what happened to them. Your job is to express that they did not deserve anything that they experienced, and that life can be different.

- Determine what they can handle emotionally. Just because they are older in age, that does not mean they are emotionally that age.

- Express permanence no matter what. They need to know that no matter what they share with you, it will not bring judgment upon them.

- Let them tell you their story, no matter how hard it is to hear. Sometimes our kids have experienced things that are unspeakable. They make us angry and want to hold someone responsible. Just listen.

- Let them cry. Just because they are fifteen years old does not mean they have passed the age of expressing their pain. Be that safe place for them where they do not have to be strong or hard.

Discussing Your Child's Story with Others

Your children's past is their story to tell, no matter their age. Do not discuss details of your kid's past that you have not first discussed with them. You are not obligated to share with anyone. Do not be afraid to correct inappropriate comments about your family or child. Over the years, I have had an array of comments regarding my family. Some were simple ignorance, some insensitive, and others downright invasive.

I was at one of my children's sports events and I had a conversation with another mom who was sitting nearby. In a roundabout way, this mom made a comparison of my kids' adoption to a family member adopting a pot-bellied pig. I was very calm, since I had been in these kinds of sticky conversations before. I boldly corrected the difference and brought the inappropriate comparison to her attention. She was embarrassed. I was less concerned about her embarrassment and more concerned about the dignity and value of my children.

Negative details of your kids' background will fuel ignorant fires and expectations society has created around fostered and adopted kids. I used to try to shield my kids from these interactions. Not anymore. I continually affirm their role and permanence in our family. They recognize when others are being inappropriate. They know that others' ignorance does not reflect on who they are.

Respectful Adoption Language (RAL) is not widely known. As foster and adoptive parents, we can use these awkward and crazy discussions as teachable moments one uninformed person at a time.

"They are all confident in the fact that they can talk in an uninhibited way with us about their history, whenever they desire."

Never introduce your children separately, using "real kids," "adopted kids," or "foster kids" to others. It will then give them permission to put stipulations on your kids or judge them differently.

Be very careful when revealing details to school officials. Teachers, neighbors, and even some family members may place a label or expectation on them that is unfair. When dealing with discipline issues at school, decide what info you want to convey. Many times, parents blame the behavior issues on the child's past, not realizing that it is setting up a cycle of excuses for the school. It also causes people to not make your child take responsibility for his/her own actions. Very few people should know the details of your child's story. It is their story to tell.

Teach Your Kids to Tell Their Own Story

If you feel a child is holding things in and it is adversely affecting their life, therapy may be a good way to get them talking. Play therapy has been proven to be effective for younger kids.

As your kids get older, they will be in situations and environments where you are not there to rescue them from others' ignorance. It is important that they feel equipped to handle these conversations on their own. Ask your kids what kinds of situations and questions make them feel uncomfortable. How do they want to answer the questions? Give them a script. Sounds crazy, but it works. Sometimes they need to know exactly what to say to defuse and exit an uncomfortable discussion. We do this with our kids for adoption, foster care, homeschooling, and other sensitive topics.

Help your kids judge the conversation and the motive of the person asking:

- Is this the right time and place for this conversation?

- Are these the appropriate people to share my story with?

- Am I comfortable around this person?

- What do I think this person will do with this information?

Years ago, one of my daughters was in a youth group. She shared with a new friend that she was adopted and a little bit about her story. The next week she came back and everyone knew her private business. She was hurt and felt betrayed. We took that opportunity to talk about relationships, trust, discretion, and our personal stories. She understood due to this experience to choose wisely when sharing such meaningful and sensitive information. Empower you child. Discussing their information with anyone should be entirely up to them. If your child wants to answer, then don't rush in to rescue them unless they seem to be getting overwhelmed or teased/bullied. Teach them to respond without anger and sarcasm but understanding of others' ignorance on the subject.

As the parent, we have to be bold and brave enough to have these discussions with our kids. They in turn will be brave enough to open up and share when they know it is a safe, non-judgmental atmosphere NO MATTER WHAT... I guarantee, if you master this, your relationship with your child will grow and flourish.

Beautiful Moments

A somber, yet beautiful moment was when we shared the entire foster care and adoption file with our two oldest kids as pre-teens. Alas, all the puzzle pieces from years of discussions were put in place.

What I Have Learned

I learned early on that each child is different. Honoring how they approach their own story made our bond with them much closer.

Prayer

Dear Lord, give me wisdom to help my child process their story. I ask you for direction to know how and when to approach this sensitive topic at every age and stage of their development. Let me exercise compassion and provide a safe place for them to feel, share, and heal.

In Jesus' Name,
Amen

"As difficult as it is to deal with angry kids, this is not a task to turn over to others. Seeking support, especially professional support, may be essential, but it doesn't replace what only you can provide."

Tricia Goyer
Calming Angry Kids

Chapter 10
Older Child Adoption

*P*reparing older kids for adoption who have never known the permanence and security of a family is not easy. Children in orphanages, or those who have been bounced around in foster care, can often develop a hardness and independence that makes family life challenging.

There are kids who have spent their entire childhood relying on no one but themselves. Imagine not being able to trust anyone, not having your needs met, being abused, neglected, or abandoned. Relying on someone else for the first time will not come easy. Often, kids will push you away to avoid rejection, because they have experienced it so many times.

RAD

Reactive Attachment Disorder is not uncommon in children who have been in foster care or an institutional setting. Children who spend more time in a setting where they are being abused, neglected, or have no loving connections to caregivers, are more likely to suffer from RAD.

This disorder has a wide spectrum of presentations from mild to extreme. It makes it very difficult to connect, show love, receive love, or trust people. Many adolescents and teens who have been in this type of setting for a long time suffer greatly. They struggle with developing relationships and accepting the care of others.

Therapy, patience, and a loving environment can guide them toward developing trust and the desire to connect with others.

Older children make up a large portion of the children waiting in orphanages and foster care for a permanent family. Many give up hope that it will happen, assuming everyone wants a baby.

There have been many efforts to bring attention to older children who are waiting. This has led to many older child adoptions both internationally, and from US foster care. Those who choose to do this must be well prepared and equipped to help their kids thrive.

How do you prepare a teen for family life? This places the foster or adoptive family in teaching mode. What the kids need is strong support and loving guidance in understanding how a family operates. These are things that need to be communicated with grace and sincerity to your new teens in words and in action.

- Rules are put in place for safety because we care.

- You can rely on us to care for you and your needs.

- We will not turn our back on you when you make a mistake.

- We genuinely want to help.

- Respect for one another builds trust.

- We are willing to listen without judgment.

- We want you to succeed and to see you reach your full potential.

"Some children have deep warrior blueprints. They have survived things that are hard to even imagine. They had protected themselves, their siblings, and sometimes their parents. Their warrior souls have difficulty resting and trusting that they are safe."
Post Institute

Sibling Group Dynamics

Older child adoption often means other siblings are involved. I have witnessed in cases across the globe where children have been responsible for other children in the absence of parents or caregivers.

Our oldest two children were joined at the hip when we adopted them. They are only fourteen months apart in age. For the first two years, it was hard to get my son to talk. His older sister did all the speaking for him. It took a lot of work and consistency to help him find his voice and to let her see that we would take care of his needs. Today he is an outspoken, confident, and driven young man with a voice of his own. He doesn't need someone to speak for him at all.

When we met our youngest three children, they had been in five homes before ours. Multiple situations failed to work out for them and here they were again, in another home. Why should they trust us at all?

The oldest of that sibling group was six when she came into our home. She spent most of her young life protecting, worrying, and "parenting" two younger children (five and three) through multiple transitions. It broke my heart that this six-year-old little girl never had a chance to be a little girl. I recall an incident early on where she was crying uncontrollably. I finally got her to calm down so that she could share what she was feeling. She was upset because both of her little brothers were misbehaving and it scared her. My daughter thought that she had to control their behavior or they would be sent to yet another home. It took a long time to convince her that this was home and their last stop NO MATTER WHAT…

"Often, kids will push you away to avoid rejection because they have experienced it so many times."

This is the same child who took a year to put her suitcase in the basement, just in case. It is a beautiful thing to see her blossom into a bold and free young lady who has had plenty of time to be a child and free from a responsibility she should not have had.

One Unit

One of the easiest things to do when adopting a sibling group is to treat them as a unit. I don't know what it is like to have one or even two children. We started with three and then jumped to six. The transitions were huge and complicated.

The important thing is to remember that, although they came together as a group, they are individual children with individual needs. One way that we have always tried to acknowledge this is with one-on-one time. Very early on in our journey as a family of eight, we realized this was crucial to each child feeling heard and valued.

If you are adopting older children or a sibling group, it will be a huge transition. Find support and other families that have done the same to help you navigate the waters.

Beautiful Moments

One of the most beautiful moments in the midst of some very hard days of transition were the many times we canceled everything on the agenda and took the whole family out for some fun. This reminded us that the most important thing was to support each other during the difficult times and support each other's healing along the way. Fun and laughter break down the barriers and stress.

What I Have Learned

I learned that hurt children need time to trust and allow you into their heart and space. We cannot force this process. In word and action, we draw closer to them over time.

Prayer

God, you brought these children into our lives. Give them back the childhood they have missed, dear God. Help us to draw closer and develop trust as we show them your love and faithfulness through our words and actions over time.

In Jesus' Name,
Amen

"The goal is to see the precious child that exists beneath the survival strategies and to let them know we see them."

Dr. Karyn Purvis

Chapter 11
Creative Discipline

*T*he best parenting advice I have ever gotten: Never hold your child accountable for something you have never taken the time to teach them.

We tend to repeat what we have seen and learned in our own childhood. Some of those things are good, and some not so good. Most of us have to learn how to parent with our children's specific needs in mind.

Your relationship with your child should never be based on their temporary behavior. They should experience your love and attention when they are at their best and worst behavior. It is imperative that we consider a child's developmental age when we are determining how to handle a situation. Children from hard places have so many hard-wired thoughts, emotions, and behaviors. However, all children who have experienced life in foster care or an orphanage do not present with all of the behaviors mentioned in this book.

Do what works for your child and your family. That may be different than the person sitting next to you. I cannot tell you how many times I have encountered a person telling me that all my children needed was a spanking. This was coming from a person observing a tantrum in a public setting, not understanding my child's background and special needs at the time.

Many years ago, I was speaking at a conference. At intermission, I happened to overhear a group of foster parents talk about one of the benefits of finalizing their adoption. It was the ability to finally spank their child. This broke my heart in a million pieces. This same foster parent had just cried during the session about the abuse this child had suffered before coming into their home. I don't think that she even realized that her actions were potentially triggering past trauma in the child she loves.

"Your relationship with your child should never be based on their temporary behavior."

I do trauma competent training all over the globe. In the US, I have found that many parents agree that finding other ways to handle challenging children is the best route to take. However, in many countries I have visited, I have been laughed to scorn when mentioning alternatives to corporal punishment. I usually entertain their point of view and dive deep into all the options they have available to them before resorting to this. By the time I finish, many are nodding their heads in agreement. I know that changing how a culture or society operates is not my responsibility. If I can help one parent who is at a loss for what to do, then I have done my job.

Spanking may stop a child in their tracks right at the moment of the offense. We have to ask ourselves if that is our only goal. Shouldn't our goal be to connect with and teach our children? Do I think parents who spank are bad parents? No. I do believe parents who rely on spanking as the FIRST reaction to every situation are lacking wisdom and guidance.

Am I saying that I have never spanked my children?
Nope. I have. It did not take long for me to realize that it
was not solving the problem. It did not shepherd my
child's heart in the right direction. It actually caused a
wall between myself and my kids that was difficult to
repair. Before considering corporal punishment, I
admonish you to look deeper at the root cause of the
behavior and come to a conclusion as to how this can be
solved while keeping your connection with your child.
Over the years we have added several disciplinary actions
to our arsenal that frequently solve the issue without
resorting to spanking.

Self-Defeating Parenting Styles

Many times, we are operating in parenting styles that are
self-destructive and are disrupting the environment and
peace in our homes.

Fear - No room for freedom or creativity. If you could,
you would keep your kids in a bubble.

Fix It - The thinking that the proper environment, proper
info, proper schools, and no negative influences will yield
perfect kids.

How Do I Look? - As long as our family looks good in the
public eye, who cares that it is falling apart at home?

Domination - Leveraging your strength and power as a
parent against your children's weaknesses.

Crowd Control - Do whatever you see everyone else
doing at the time.

Patch Work - **Patching up problems as they arise** instead of intentional parenting.

Emergency - Parenting only takes place when something goes horribly wrong.

Discipline vs Punishment

Discipline - is a teaching opportunity. Talking to your child should always come before anything else. Sometimes your children need help articulating their thoughts and feelings about the situation. Discipline should always be age appropriate.

Punishment - making a child suffer or pay for their behavior. Punishing a child for behavior that is not "age appropriate" is counterproductive. Forget their age…what is their stage?

Spanking and hurtful words can cause more harm than good. Many times, you will end up with the same or worse behavior than before.

"Our children need to know they are precious in the sunshine and in the rain."
Dr. Karyn Purvis

Time Out vs Time In

Time out

Means I am not acknowledging you or the reasons behind why you are having a hard time following instructions. Although there are some times where time alone to think and ponder are warranted, there are many times we do this just to rid the environment of the "problem" at the moment, not getting to the real issues.

Time In
Sometimes drawing the child in closer will solve the
problem. You will begin to notice that the reason they are
acting out in some ways is because of lack of attention to
the problem, fears, or behavior.

When your children have experienced trauma in the form
of abuse and neglect, using corporal punishment can be
counterproductive, and it can reawaken those same fears.
Fight, Flight, or Freeze reactions are hard to overcome.
What is at the core of the issue? How can you help your
child deal with this issue more productively?

Do Not Engage
Why does engaging the child in the middle of a meltdown
make things worse? A child who has gone into fight mode
will accelerate if you engage in the same behavior and go
"there" with them. The best thing to do is to remain calm
and present.

*"Withdrawing love when their behavior is challenging
gives children the message that our love depends on what
they do. Eventually, they will believe they are only worthy
of love when they act in ways that are convenient or
prescribed by others. Their fierce hearts will tame, their
minds will obey, their spirits will dim, and the essence of
them will fade. Limits enforced with love will teach.
Limits without love will shame."*
Karen Young

We have a child who was full of rage when he came into
our home. The word that set him off was "no." We did
what all the parenting books told us to do. Of course, we
thought that sending him to his room was the perfect

idea. It got rid of the noise and removed all the drama from the situation, right? Wrong! We could very easily engage, scream, and turn it into an hour-long drama-filled fit with no conclusion. Our answer was just as bad for this particular kid. Sending him away reinforced his fear of being abandoned and pushed away. It sent him into a fitful rage that lasted one and a half hours; if the walls of his bedroom could talk. He became destructive and hard to manage.

"When your children have experienced trauma in the form of abuse and neglect, using corporal punishment can be counterproductive, and it can reawaken those same fears."

One change to how we handled the situation made all the difference. We pulled close instead of sending him away. His ungodly long raging fits went from one and a half hours to five minutes. What did we do? We sat with him in his disappointment, speaking calmly or not at all. Our presence and reassurance of our love even when he was angry made all the difference. Handing him a book or watching a show with him quietly helped him to regroup and deal with his emotions, often ending in a hug and a smile before rejoining his siblings. Today, he has learned how to handle the word "no." Does he like it? Not at all, but he can handle it. He also can handle having a moment in his room to regroup on days when he is struggling to make good choices. This happened over time and with reassurance of our love for him NO MATTER WHAT...

We had to do the hard thing. It takes time and dedication to try new things. Every plan does not work for every child. You have to find what works for yours.

Parenting with grace has become my goal. I think of how God has grace with me when I am not obedient or miss the mark. How can we extend that same kind of grace to our children?

- Why are we having this problem?

- What can be learned from this?

- How can I creatively teach a lesson without humiliating my child?

- How can I model what they can do better next time?

"When little people are overwhelmed by big emotions, it's our job to share our calm. Not join their chaos."
L.R. Knost

Fear-Based Behaviors

Lying – Fear of what will happen if they tell the truth. The human response to fear as a consequence of truth is often lying. If you have a child who lies often, it is probably because of the response that they have gotten in the past from those in authority over them. If that response was scary, painful, and threatening, a lie seems safer. Developing a safe place to be honest with the good, the bad, and the ugly, is the best place to start when it comes to lying.

Hitting – Fight response to offense or fear. A child who is using violence to communicate has not learned how to solve problems. They have a hard time attaching words or feelings to their present state of mind. Work with your children on developing a name for their feeling and helping them express themselves in a way that gets them the results they want. Role play is always helpful.

Defiance – Fear that there is no one they can trust. Many times, defiance comes from the dismissal of their feelings and needs by those who should care. If they reject authority in all forms, it may be because they have been let down. *Why should I care if no one else does*?, is often the feeling. They will try to push people away before they can be rejected themselves.

Practice listening and asking your child how you can help. Show you care about the little things, and often the feelings they have will change, and the behavior as well. This may not have anything to do with how you interact with them. Sometimes it is based on their past and the things they have experienced long before you entered the picture.

> *"Practice listening and asking your child how you can help."*

Stealing – Fear that their needs will not be met. Many kids feel that they deserve what someone else has, and the only way to obtain it is by taking it. There are some children, however, who enjoy the thrill of getting away with stealing. Help them understand the consequences of this escalated behavior leading to interactions with law enforcement. Small infractions lead to large ones when they are not corrected and held accountable for them. Be vigilant and consistent with your response to stealing and the destruction of others' property.

Anger – Holding on to adverse feelings that build over time. Much of the time, anger comes from sadness and disappointment that festers. Talking through those disappointments and allowing them to grieve will be a start to a new perspective.

Verbal Abuse – Pushing people away with words that often describe how they feel about themselves. "I hate you," "I hate my life," and "I wish you never adopted me." These words are every parent's nightmare. Your child is trying to communicate something underneath these words. It is the only way they know how to let the pain out. It is important to model kind and calm words in the heat of the battle. It is usually more about how they feel about themselves and less of a personal attack on you.

"In my book When Your Kid is Hurting, *there are Four Goals of Misbehavior, one being ATTENTION. A child only feels worthy when they have been noticed, even if it is for bad behavior. Secondly, POWER. A child may only feel good about themselves when they have exercised power over a person or situation. Third would be REVENGE. This is when a child wants others to hurt the way that they have been hurt. The fourth goal is DISPLAY OF INADEQUACY. You may have a child that feels useless where they feel trying to do anything right is fruitless."*
Dr. Kevin Lehman

As foster or adoptive parents to a traumatized child, part of our life is decoding the behavior and feelings of children who have not been able to express them. The other part is figuring out what works for each child to help them develop healthy behaviors, clear thoughts, and a positive future.

I have several examples from my own parenting journey that made me dig deep and investigate why a child was behaving the way they were, and what we did to help them.

"It's not uncommon for children from hard places to struggle with the feeling of sadness. See, while anger is a protective emotion, sadness is a signaling emotion that helps draw people in. Anger says, 'Stay away or else' and sadness says, 'Please come close, I need help'."
Stephanie Grant

We have been homeschooling our children for eleven years. You can imagine all that goes into homeschooling six children. One of my kids spent hours crying over copy work when he was about seven years old. I simply labeled it as lazy and that he wanted to get out of doing the work. When it went on for months, I had to pay attention. I had to dig deeper into what was really happening under the surface. We recognized he had dysgraphia. It is a challenge with writing and the use of his hands when doing micro tasks. This child is very bright, so we knew it was not cognitive. His mind was moving too fast for his hands to keep up. This resulted in headaches and severe pain in his hands. Thankfully, we dug deeper so that we could help him. We refocused on helping him with multiple accommodations to share his intelligence with the world in other ways while practicing his writing in short stints. What if we stuck with the lazy narrative? It would have affected our relationship with our child and his self-esteem, as well as his success overall. He was not misbehaving; he needed help and did not know how to express that.

There was a time when another one of my sons told outlandish lies continually on a sibling that caused a lot of tension in our home. It took a while for us to really dissect the reasons behind the lies. The conclusion was fear. He felt manipulated and controlled by this sibling. He felt that if he lied on them often enough, it would keep him from having to interact with them. We dealt with it on both sides with compassion and wisdom. When the truth was revealed, we were able to deal with the real problem. The lying was not the problem. It was just a symptom of the real problem, which was based on fear.

"He was not misbehaving; he needed help and did not know how to express that."

Several of my children have had issues with food hoarding. In the beginning, we always thought it was an issue with stealing. It took a serious revelation for us to get to the bottom of the reasoning. For children who have been starved, malnourished, or neglected, the fear of never having enough to eat is ingrained in their subconscious mind. They were not stealing, they were storing up food out of fear that they would not have their needs met, much like their lives before they joined our family. Healing began when we recognized the REAL root of the behavior: fear.

As you can see in my examples above, fear was the root of every behavior, and, dare I say it, it is the root of most of the behaviors you may be seeing in your children. Give an answer to their fears and many times the behavior will taper or disappear altogether.

Subconscious Behaviors

Have you had to deal with weapons of mass destruction? No, we are not talking about war. We are talking about your home. Kids who have felt completely out of control in their lives often use urine, feces, and the lack of bodily care as a weapon of control…even older children.

We have had our share of pee and poop bombs over the years and it always came down to one of these three reasons. Many times, these actions can be a sign of a deeper cry for help resulting from sexual abuse. This is something to investigate further, possibly with a therapist, if you are not sure how to handle it. Other times this behavior can be linked to a physical problem that may need to be checked out by your pediatrician. A possible third reason you are seeing this behavior may be a child who is acting out in the only area they feel they can control. In this case, giving the child some say in neutral areas throughout their day may help them feel like they have some control.

"Give an answer to their fears and many times the behavior will taper or disappear altogether."

Lack of body care is another common issue in foster care and other traumatized kids. Much of it is linked to self-esteem and self-worth. If a child came from an environment where they were abused in many ways, neglected, or abandoned, taking care of their body would not be a priority. The most effective way of handling this is education, compassion, persistence, and modeling good self-care practices as parents.

I would love to say that we got these things right the first time. Often, we were on the wrong track and had to rely on God and educating ourselves to turn things around in our home. The best thing we can do as parents is to admit what is working and what isn't working. Apologize and talk to your child about how you would like to handle things in the future. Make a concerted effort to try new things that will lighten the atmosphere and express more grace as your child works through issues possibly related to prior trauma.

- Provide a solution to your child's fear.

- Model/teach them how to handle their emotions.

- Choose consequences that are not verbally, emotionally, or physically abusive.

- Focus MORE on who they are and who they have the potential to be than the current behavior.

Ideas for Discipline – These are ideas that bring connection and teaching moments instead of humiliation and punishment.

- Spend extra alone time with them

- Conversation about their feelings

- Extra chores

- Early bedtime

- Correcting the error or problem

- Free time swapped for something else

- Electronic time swapped for something else

- Item in question removed (careful with this one with children who are attached to something emotionally)

- Bible study on the topic

- Doing chores for the child whom they offended

- Doing an activity/project with the child who they have been bickering/fighting with

Beautiful Moments

In many of the behavioral situations in our home, the most beautiful moments were when we helped our children name their feelings. They finally felt heard and understood.

What I Have Learned

I have learned to allow God in the spaces of correction that bring me and my child closer instead of further apart. One of the greatest things I learned was that the yelling and spanking I tried in the past was the least effective way to handle their behavior and model self-regulation.

Prayer

Father, forgive me for the times I rushed in to fix my child's behavior without consulting you. Teach me, dear Lord, how to connect with my child in a way that causes fear to leave. Help me to bring them to a place of healing and deal with the root of the issues they are facing without causing further pain.

In Jesus' Name,
Amen

"When a child flirts or is sexually precocious, he/she may be trying to express this: This was what I was trained to do because I was sexually abused by caregivers. Inappropriate sexuality was the only way I ever got positive attention when I was younger. I don't know how else to please people."

Dr. Karyn Purvis

Chapter 12
Aftermath of Sexual Abuse

*T*he school bus pulled up in front of her house. Like usual, my aunt came out to meet me and walk me in. My mom was a struggling single mom and I was a half-day kindergartner. My aunt was the only childcare option she had for me at the time. After all, it was safe since it was family.

Like most days after school, I sat at the table doing crafts in the cold kitchen with black and white checkered tile. This was a huge, historic home. She had so many kids, I could not keep track. There were her biological kids…ten of them. Then there was a revolving door of foster youth and toddlers from time to time. The weird thing is, she was never there. She was a nurse, so she worked long hours and slept the rest of the time.

How could a child feel so alone and vulnerable in a house full of people? I would stare at the basement steps that seemed like they led to a deep dark dungeon. All I knew was that periodically one of her teenage sons would appear at the door. Today was one of those days. He made eye contact with me and discreetly told me to follow him. I was five years old and he was fifteen. I was supposed to follow his instructions. I followed him into the beautiful downstairs bathroom with an antique pedestal sink and floral wallpaper. What happened that day in that bathroom changed my life forever. My view of relationships, men, intimacy, sex, and love was forever changed in one day. What just happened to me? I was only five years old. A baby.

Looking back on that moment, the details of that day are still fresh. The coldness of the house, the smells, the absence of anyone to protect me in a house full of people. I spent my youth recreating that experience in my mind and in relationships with promiscuity and curiosity. I am so grateful to have married a wonderful man who helped me understand love, intimacy, and what a godly relationship was supposed to be like.

"What happened that day in that bathroom changed my life forever."

Thirty-nine years later, I stand on the other side of the fence. As a mom, I have found myself being overly protective and dogmatic about my kids' safety. My children were exposed to unspeakable things. Who better to understand and help them through it, right?

I was guarded about writing this story, because it is so personal, and I wanted to protect my extended family. However, the things I share can help children and the foster/adoptive parents who love them.

If you have witnessed any of the following behaviors in your child, they **may** be a sign of prior sexual abuse or physical abuse. They need to be taken seriously.

- Unusual preoccupation with genitalia (their own or others')
- Daytime and/or bedtime wetting
- Smearing or playing with feces
- Night terrors
- Fear of certain people or genders

- Inappropriate play
- Promiscuity
- Alienation and secrecy
- Body image issues

How do I help my child? Where do I start? What if they are acting out sexually? HELP! I understand your frustration, your anger, and desperation to help your child heal and overcome. To do this, you must approach the matter from three perspectives: Compassion, Structure and Therapy.

Compassion

The worst thing we can do as parents of sexually abused children is assume that the fears, sexual behaviors, and residual effects will go away because they are now in a loving, safe environment. It does not go away and it won't unless it is addressed and diligently worked on over time. You might ask, "How much time?" As long as it takes. Months, years, or a lifetime. NO MATTER WHAT...

I look at my children when they struggle with any number of trauma-related behaviors and embrace the innocence behind their experience. When you made the commitment to your child, you were in it for the good, the bad, and the ugly. Recognize that if your child is acting out as a result of the abuse they have suffered, IT IS NOT THEIR FAULT. It may be hard to accept, but compassion must take over for them to thrive. You must provide an emotionally and physically safe environment for all the children in your home.

- Give them power over their own body. Asking permission to help them dress or bathe helps them to understand that their body is their own and they are in control of it.

- Having consistent talks with them about not touching others and not allowing others to touch them is imperative.

- It is important that shame is not used as a tactic for fears or impulses they have not learned to control. They are not the evil perpetrator, they are victims.

- As they grow, have continual discussions about proper intimacy and sexual education on their level.

- Have an open-door policy for them to talk to you about anything.

- Even if the child has to be separated temporarily for a variety of reasons, it is important to take time out as a parent with the child for bonding. Never make them feel alienated, unloved, or separate from the rest of the family.

Structure

Compassion without structure leaves too much room for curiosity. Structure without compassion is cold and pointless. Your child needs both. I am sad to say I had neither from my parents because it was kept a secret. Prior sexual abuse can cause a child to act out in ways that can offend others and/or cause them to become a perpetrator themselves. While protecting them from further abuse, you must also protect others from their curiosity as they progress and heal. Not every child who experiences sexual abuse acts out sexually. Some act out from their own pain and confusion due to the abuse.

"It does not go away and it won't unless it is addressed and diligently worked on over time."

You must be diligent in providing a structured environment that keeps everyone safe from harm.

- Dressing, bathing, and other personal moments must be guarded as private.

- Children who trigger similar behaviors in each other should not share rooms or be left alone under any circumstances. This may take creativity, but it is very important.

- Everyone in the home must know, understand, and abide by the structures set in place for safety.

- Mandatory Reporting is important in any family. When something inappropriate is seen, heard, or experienced, the parents need to be alerted immediately.

- Sleepovers for children struggling with sexual behaviors may not be a good idea unless an adult is present at ALL times, even sleeping hours.

- Baby monitors work well to ensure everyone's safety.

- Pay close attention to your children during play time and conversations they have with siblings. It can be a clue as to what thoughts are dominating their mind.

Therapy

I used to think that therapy was for wimps. Now, I wish that someone would have provided me with therapy as a child. It took many years, heartache, experiences, and work to overcome the trauma I experienced that could have been alleviated. You must be willing to do whatever it takes to help your child thrive and overcome this trauma.

- Choose a therapist or counselor who you trust and who comes highly recommended by other parents.

- Choose a therapist who has experience in foster care, adoption, and trauma.

- Meet with the therapist in advance to develop a rapport and understand their philosophy.

- Choose a therapist who holds your family's values.

- Choose play therapy for younger or special needs children.

- Request that you be present for therapy until you are comfortable with the progress.

With your help and diligence, your child can thrive and grow. Your commitment to their healing and progress will make all the difference in their lives, future relationships, and life choices. You can do this!

Beautiful Moments

The look on a child's face when they know they are safe
and that you will fight to protect them no matter what.
That is a beautiful moment.

What I Have Learned

I have learned that you have to keep your cool and deal
with things calmly if you want your children to tell you
things that are hard to share.

Prayer

Dear God, help me to operate in compassion, wisdom,
and truth when listening to my children. Guide me
through the maze of pain that envelops them due to their
experiences. Let me be used by you to bring healing and
wholeness to their bodies and hearts, Father.

In Jesus' Name,
Amen

"My child doesn't remember being hungry as a baby, but his body does…"

Foster2Forever

Chapter 13
Food Fight

"*M*om, when you hide food from me to keep me from hoarding food, aren't you in fact…HOARDING FOOD?"

I thought to myself, "Idiot, what are you doing?" Hearing my child say this made me realize that everything we were doing was perpetuating our children's fear. We thought we had it all figured out. We were doing what we needed to do to fix this problem of food hoarding.

A few of our children experienced much more trauma than others and the evidence was showing years later. I was worried. I was confused. I was frustrated. They are safe now and they have everything they need to thrive. Food was coming up missing in massive quantities. We were finding extremely creative hiding places for the evidence. We were furious. "We don't teach you to steal!" "That is not proper behavior!"

We had no idea what to do or how to handle our child's need to hoard and take food. We slowly began to understand that this was not a "stealing" issue. Our child was not trying to take anything from the rest of the family. This was purely an innate reaction to fear not even they understood.

"We thought we had it all figured out."

Going back eight years, I began to put together the pieces of what we were now seeing. Rereading all my early reports that we received on our precious babies, things became clear. My sweet little child had been deprived of any solid foods for the first two years of life, laid in a bed and fed a bottle of water, and left alone for hours, sometimes days. As a mother now, I cannot even imagine a child surviving that.

So even though we now understood the why, we still did not know the how. How do we help our child work through this fear into freedom? Will there be a day when the paralyzing fear of not having your basic needs met will ever be quenched? My child was three when the adoption was final. We were still fighting this fear when our baby turned eleven.

The Scene of the Crime

Seventy-three packages of fruit snacks were hidden under the bed, in toy boxes, and in closets. Over one hundred Slim Jims were hidden in the closets, drawers, heating vents, and planted in other siblings' rooms.

When we brought home three more kids, it never crossed my mind that one child's trauma and past would be a trigger to another. We arranged the rooms according to age and gender and decorated with the best of the best. Within two months, we began to see odd eating patterns. A few of the kids were not eating like normal. Later it was discovered that they were saving their food.

Together they devised a plan to save, transport, hide, and split their spoils in their room. This went on for quite a while before we caught on. One day as I was spring cleaning, I found one wrapper, then two, then ten, then molded orange peels. "Go up to your room, and reveal to me where you have all of the food hidden immediately!"

What we found was amazing! I was dumbfounded at their creativity, yet angry.

How can a child who has been in a stable, loving home for eight years with all their needs and desires met need to hoard food? The answer is complex and simple all at once. This fear and need to gather was hard wired long before we met them. All of our children endured circumstances of neglect where many of their basic needs were not met before coming home. We became increasingly concerned when we noticed non-food items were being eaten as well. We found chewed-up toilet paper, plaster, plastic, yarn, rubber, pencils, and other items. We knew we needed to help them but did not know what to do. In the beginning we did it ALL wrong. Many parents are doing the same things.

"When a child hoards food, he/she may be trying to express this: I was painfully hungry and undernourished and nearly starved before, and I am haunted by the fear it will happen again."
Dr. Karyn Purvis

Under Lock & Key
We did everything we could think of to stop this madness. Here are the things that DID NOT WORK!

Punishment
Punishment unrelated to the actual offense is counterproductive. The child is not going to stop hoarding because you dish out heavy punishments. Punishment only treats the symptom of the problem, but it never gets at the issues that cause the behavior. It also

puts a wedge between you and your child, which does not help with bonding. This was the worst thing ever. Time-out, losing privileges, and being sent to their room was not the answer and it caused my relationship with my children to drift apart. That is not what I wanted.

Locks

What is this, a prison? No, it is a home. The fact that we thought this was going to solve the problem is laughable in hindsight. What are locks for? To limit the access to something we deem valuable. Why does my child have this issue in the first place? In their early years, they did not have access to the nutrition and care they needed. Many foster and adoptive homes use this as a method to stop the hoarding. All it does is keep them from taking food, but it does not help them deal with the trauma related behavior and heal. After all, healing is what we want, right? My children were hurt by this and became more fearful as a result. Locking things up made their fear worse and their actions desperate.

"Will there be a day when the paralyzing fear of not having your basic needs met will ever be quenched?"

Hiding Food

What is food hoarding, anyway? Hiding and stashing food with the fear that there will be a shortage or lack of access in the future. "Mom, when you hide food from me to keep me from hoarding food, aren't you in fact… HOARDING FOOD?" I was teaching my child to hoard food by hoarding it myself. That was such an eye-opening moment for me. My children became more creative and investigative. They always found what they wanted and when they found it, they cleaned it out!

Kitchen Ban

This is just ridiculous. The kitchen is the hub of most American homes. It was exhausting trying to impose such a ridiculous thing. Banning a child from the kitchen is insane. At some point they will need to go in the kitchen. Trying to police such nonsense as a parent is putting yourself in prison. Just stop it!

Breaking Free

When you know better, you do better! Thankfully it did not take long for us to "get it." When you have a child who is dealing with such fears and it is affecting everything in the home, you need to stop and evaluate the source. Only then can you come to a point of actually helping them. Sometimes the source of the tension is the parent. I know that is not easy to hear or accept, but it is true. Your reaction to this type of behavior or any other behavior can make or break the situation. No one is going to get it right 100% of the time. A good parent makes mistakes and says sorry a lot. They are also dogmatic about doing better next time the situation presents itself. I had to apologize to my children for my response to the struggle they were having. I felt horrible that I did not see the issue for what it really was: FEAR! I took it Offensively, as if they were doing something to me. It was quite the contrary. One day I called them into the kitchen, and I had a talk with them about the issues we were having. It was heartfelt and it was the beginning of healing.

"I know that people have promised all of you lots of things and have not done them. I know that there were times when you did not eat and get the food you needed. It may not be easy to trust this mommy and daddy to do anything different. We promise you that you will never go without food. If you find it hard to trust us for the future, I ask you to do one thing...just trust us today. Then when you wake up tomorrow, decide to trust us again. Let's take it day, by day, by day. Can I get you guys to do that?"

Tears fell, a few smiled, and others asked questions about food. I felt I had conquered my attitude regarding the situation and now I could help my kids with their issues. The things I suggest may seem simple, and you may say they won't work. All I ask you to do is try them for an extended period of time. Don't give up at the slightest relapse.

Let's look at some things that can help your child through this very rough spot. You will find the answers are much closer than you ever imagined: right in the kitchen!

Healthy Foods Available
The first thing we did was take all the locks off the snack cupboards, stopped hiding (hoarding) food from them, and lifted the kitchen ban. This helped take away a lot of fear and stress on everyone in the home. The last thing we wanted to do was add to the trauma they had already suffered before joining our family.

We have a way of handling snacks in our home that gives them freedom, choices, and power over what they eat and when. When they were younger, we had six snack sacks hanging on the wall in the kitchen with each of their names on them. They were filled after breakfast every day with a rotating group of snacks. They could have these snacks at any time of the day as well as an unlimited amount of assorted fruits from a bowl on the counter that was refilled daily. We always made sure that the snacks we chose were healthier choices and not junk. Having unlimited fatty and sugary food available will cause an entirely different food issue.

Recognizing Triggers

Recognizing the triggers that your kids have is half the battle. You will begin to notice that you can set a clock by your child's responses to life circumstances. Prepare accordingly to help them through it. Hoarding only takes place in secret. When you notice your child drawing inward and away from you and the family, those may be the best times to draw them closer to help them learn coping skills such as trust and communication. The more I started to use the "time-in" technique with my kids when they were having trouble, they had less time to meditate on and act upon those lurking fears.

Food Preparation

Once we got our children involved in the kitchen, many of their fears diminished. From grocery shopping, putting the food away, helping to plan menus, preparing food with parents, and choosing their own snacks, it gives them the power they need. They will begin to see that even when food is getting low, you faithfully replace it. Our child who dealt with this fear the most has actually become quite the chef. We watch cooking shows together and dream up new dishes. They are looking at food differently.

Consequences

Children should not be punished or shamed because of this behavior. It will cause them to become more secretive and bitter. However, there should be consequences for behavior that affects others in the home. If a child is taking a majority of a certain item from someone else, a consequence is in order. We have made them do the other child's chores, or they miss out on that one item the next time snack bags are filled. Healthy and just consequences are the key. Never shame, punish, or deal with them out of anger. Sometimes this is easier said than done.

"When you notice your child drawing inward and away from you and the family, those may be the best times to draw them closer to help them learn coping skills."

Communication

Talk to your child. Many times, the things we think are bothering them are far from the real problem. Develop a rapport where they feel comfortable talking about their feelings instead of eating them. Your children should be confident in your desire to provide what they need. I am embarrassed to admit that our kids were afraid to ask for more food at the table. We cannot remember when or how we gave them that impression. Not anymore. Asking for seconds at dinner should not be a scary event. We tell our kids to speak up and ask for what they want. Now they know they are free to get more and enjoy their meals without fear.

Deflect Attention

Completely deflect attention from the issue. Don't continue to point it out or harp on it constantly. It may take weeks, months, or even years for them to turn the situation completely around. Your job is to help them understand the source, provide support, and help them manage the fear. There are adults who still have to discipline themselves to move past these issues due to childhood fears. It takes time and support! We address the issue and move on.

Therapy

Sometimes you are doing all the right things and the progress is very slow. There may be a need for a third party to see and perceive things you cannot. This is especially necessary if your child is consuming non-food items.

They are all older now at the ages of 17, 16, 13, 13, 12, and 10. Everyone has full access to cooking, snacks, and fruit throughout the day. We instituted a Dinner Boss position in our home. This gives everyone the opportunity throughout the week to plan, prepare, and serve a meal for the family. It develops confidence in a crucial life skill. It also helps instill confidence that food will always be there. We no longer have the snack packs. We have no more inhibitions, minimal fear, and minimal hoarding surrounding food. Does this mean there are not temptations or that their fear does not rear its ugly head from time to time? No. It just does not control my kids or my household anymore.

There is hope! This behavior is very common in children who have been neglected. It takes time to help them through it and to rid their little hearts of that fear. I am thrilled with the progress my children have made. Most of all, the changes that we made as parents have made the biggest and most dramatic improvement. It is important to deal with the issues your children have, but the most important thing is to maintain a loving and supportive relationship. You are just the parent for the job.

Beautiful Moments

It is a beautiful moment to see the very children that were riddled with fear overcome this behavior with confidence and become amazing chefs in their own right.

What I Have Learned

I have learned to grant my children grace in areas that are hard wired into them due to their past trauma.

Prayer

Lord, let my children always look to you as their provider. Let their confidence be in your word and your promises to them. Allow them to trust us, as their parents, to manifest your word in the form of their needs in this home.

In Jesus' Name,
Amen

"We do not need to know the entire beginning of a child's story to change the ending."

Fi Newood

Chapter 14
Teens & Letting Go

I have not adopted kids as teens; however, I am now parenting four teens and two preteens. Much of the experiences they had before joining our family still affect them and come out in multiple ways today.

I would not be the first parent to observe my teen's extraordinary resistance to my wisdom and warnings based on my own mistakes as a youth. God's word says that we are to train our children in the ways of the Lord and when they are old, they will not depart. He does not promise us that there will not be hiccups, mistakes, and mountains to climb on the way.

"They have to choose God and His ways for themselves. My job is to expose them to the things of God, the word of God, and to model God's ways for them."

I remember before I had children, I was the best parent ever. Any time I saw teens misbehave or go astray, I looked directly at the parent. Are there things that we can do to avoid our child's life being a complete train wreck? Of course there are. However, we are all responsible for our own choices in life.

What I have learned over the years is that my children are free-will agents. They have to choose God and His ways for themselves. My job is to expose them to the things of God, the word of God, and to model God's ways for them. Do you know how hard of a revelation that was for me? I wanted to be able to orchestrate this perfectly straight path toward success and righteousness. It does not work that way. I have to do my job and allow God to do His work in and through them.

I have met many foster and adoptive parents who have been hurt and absolutely blown away by the choices that their children have made, not realizing that the thinking and behavior they are witnessing has been so deeply ingrained in that child. It takes time and a lot of patience and compassion to see them through the really tough stuff.

"We stress about the future in an effort to avoid something that happened in the past, all while missing the gifts of the present."
Post Institute

I was heartbroken for a dear family that had to consider placing one of their children in out-of-home care. They tried everything. They needed to trust professionals and God with their child's care when they were at the end of their rope. I remember thinking to myself, "How can a parent make a decision like that?" Until I was that parent.

After managing extreme behaviors for years, we had to make a similar decision for one of our children. It is literally one of the most difficult choices a parent could be faced with. To hand your child over to someone else and trust that they will be okay can keep you up at night...and it did. It was absolutely terrifying. In the words of a dear friend and confidant, "Things will work out okay, or they won't." Whether things happen the way we want for our child or not, we will be a safe place to land. We will be praying and guiding them from the sidelines.

I spent too many years stressed and confused as to how to help my child. The older my baby got, the more intense the situation became, and I knew that if we did not do something quick and drastic, it would destroy our family and the peace of our home.

At the writing of this book, my child has been away from home for six months. It has been hard to not have direct access and control over my kid's day-to-day life. The guilt that tries to creep in is excruciating. The sadness that tried to overtake me became unbearable. What I dreamed for my child during their teen years…squashed. I had to stop homeschooling this particular kid in the eleventh grade, after having them home for ten years. I had to trust them to a system that threatened to break them.

> *"Treat the child as though he already is the person he's capable of becoming."*
> *Haim Ginott*

However, there is good news. My relationship with this child is better than it has ever been since we brought them home as a toddler. I see God weaving a bond I always prayed for as absence draws us closer. They are succeeding in their grades and pursuing a Culinary Arts Certificate toward a pursuit of a lifelong dream.

This is hard stuff. Teens go through a lot during those crucial years. You add trauma, abuse, and neglect in the early years to the mix, and it becomes a firestorm that only God can put out. I don't regret making the decision that I did. I trust God in the end that we will see His faithfulness in our child's life. This was the best thing for our child's healing and maturity. So, I remind my children regularly of who God created them to be, even when we see behavior that speaks otherwise. We exercise compassion and remain a safe place for our child to land when things get rough, as they often do. No matter what their choices are, we will love them unconditionally.

I write about my process of dealing with control issues in my book *LET GO!* I learned how to lean on God when I did not have the answers and nothing I did in my own strength was working.

Sometimes letting go and allowing our children to take full responsibility for their actions is crucial. As parents, we want to keep them in a bubble and even shield them from the consequences of their own actions. That is not parenting, it is enabling. Letting go is a process. I get better and better at it as the time goes on.

"Don't be too quick to jump in and fix the situation. It's a natural instinct, but fight the urge."
Dr. Kevin Lehman

Aging Out

After adopting our youngest three children in 2013, we considered adopting two teens (15 and 16 years old) who had spent their lives in foster care. They were prize students, athletes, and all-around good kids based on their profile. We were really excited about the prospect of getting to know them. I took a shot in the dark and sent a request to their case worker. About two weeks later, I received an email that greatly saddened me. However, knowing trauma, I understood what I was reading.

The brother and sister felt they had each other and had weathered many storms together. They no longer wanted to be adopted. They asked for their profile to be removed from the website and decided to simply age out of foster care. The gravity of that statement... "I don't want or need parents in my life, I can do this all on my own," had to have come from a great place of pain. Having been let down by so many people for so long, looking forward to another disappointment did not feel worth the fight.

This particular sibling group seemed to have a vision and was motivated with a plan for their lives. I always think about them and pray that things work out well for them. The unfortunate truth is that they may be an anomaly. Most kids that spend their entire life in foster care without permanence and stability have an extremely difficult time adjusting to adulthood.

A sad reality for teens in foster care and in orphanages around the world is that it does not last forever. When these impressionable youth turn the age of adulthood, which is different depending upon the country, they are sent out into the world. Prepared or not, they are forced to deal with the responsibilities of adulthood without much training, education, or connection.

My heart aches for any kid who is not ready. The life that awaits is not promising unless someone has invested heavily in them prior to adulthood. I have never agreed that children should suddenly be thrust into life at the age of sixteen or eighteen. The maturity level, ability to support oneself, and survive may be different for every young adult. This does not mean we should baby our children and do everything for them. It simply means invest in preparing foster youth for a successful adulthood. It doesn't just happen. It has to be intentional. The best thing we can do is resist the urge to rescue them, while being a guide.

Beautiful Moments

I remember the moment my child called and told me that they missed me and just wanted to talk. I waited fourteen years to hear those words. It was a beautiful moment.

What I Have Learned

I have learned that doing hard things is not easy, but it's always rewarding on the other side of God's instruction.

Prayer

Lord, Let me model a righteous life before my kids. Give me the wisdom to do my part in raising them to love and serve you. Protect my child during those times that they are not following you. Father, I trust my child with you. You know better than I do what they need and how to bring them to a place of repentance and healing. God, I release control and allow you to work in and through my child's life.

In Jesus' Name,
Amen

"Unless someone like you cares a whole awful lot, nothing is going to get better. It's not."

Dr. Seuss, The Lorax

Chapter 15
Greatest Advocate

*I*f not you, then who? This is the question foster and adoptive parents need to ask themselves. Called to be agents of healing, we also have to be advocates for our kids in every possible area.

When we see a need arise or a challenge appear, we must jump to it. No differently than if our biological children are struggling, we must be their greatest advocate.

When children come into care or are adopted from an institutional setting, there will be challenges. Some kids will have greater challenges than others. When you bring your child home or as soon as placement happens, start observing and taking notes. Early intervention for any challenge is crucial.

> *"Feelings are feelings. They are not right or wrong."*
> *Dr. Kevin Leman*

Look for a therapist in your area who is familiar with trauma, foster care, adoption, and working with children/ youth. The therapist you choose should also have practices that line up with your beliefs and values.

Depression

There is a difference between depression and a short-term sadness due to a life event. If you see a perpetual sadness in your child that does not give way to enjoyment or peace at all, it is cause for concern. Get help immediately!

Medical Care

Many children in care need someone to advocate for medical interventions, medication, and therapies. When they are in your care, you are the person who knows them better than anyone. You can observe the reaction to medications, sleeping patterns, physical ailments, and other medical needs. You must stand up and be bold to make sure your kids get the treatment, therapy, medicine, and care they need to thrive.

Unmanageable Behaviors

As we discussed in previous chapters, behavioral issues are a clue to a much deeper root. Therapy can help get to the bottom of some of these destructive patterns.

Out-of-Home Care

There are organizations and programs across the US, and possibly in your country, that provide therapeutic care for children that need a different atmosphere to heal and deal with specific challenges. If your child was adopted through foster care in the US, it is possible that your state offers funds to help with this kind of program. Do your homework and make sure you are aware of all of your options.

Educational Needs

You may have a child who struggles in school for any number of reasons. You are the only person who can make sure they get the accommodations that they need to have a fair chance at succeeding in a school setting.

Research IEPs and 504 plans to understand what your role is versus the roles of each person on your child's team. Know what options are available to your child and push for the maximum accommodation possible.

Most school districts will offer testing for children with learning differences or Dyslexia, Dysgraphia, Dyscalculia, and many physical challenges. If the district does not cover the full cost of this testing, the state may offer financial assistance if your child was adopted through foster care in the US.

In all of these areas, it is important to dig for all of the possible programs and local assistance that you can find. Make sure you are familiar with what is available through local and state agencies. Your kids need you to do what they cannot do for themselves.

You have to be dogmatic when advocating for them. You must keep knocking on doors and making phone calls until you get a yes for the help your child needs to flourish.

Beautiful Moment

It was a beautiful moment when I was informed that medical assistance was available from the state for three of my children who needed it. The answer to that prayer was on the other end of a phone call.

What I Have Learned

I learned not to accept NO when it comes to the needs of my kids. Make one more call.
One more visit.

Prayer

Lord, help me to be my child's greatest advocate. Thank you, Lord, for placing people in our lives who can guide us through red tape to get the services we need for our child. Guide us to the right therapists, doctors, teachers, and advocates to help us provide the very best care for them.

In Jesus' Name,
Amen

"The children are the curriculum."

Lisa Murphy

Chapter 16
Learning Environments

I have noticed over the years that many homeschool families and foster and adoptive families overlap. Often parents recognize that the compassion, relaxed atmosphere, and flexibility in learning works well for kids who have dealt with trauma and many of its effects.

Homeschooling may not be something that every family can do, or even want to do. However, as a parent, I would investigate the options in your area that would allow for interest-led or a strengths-based approach in learning. Every child can benefit from being highlighted for what they do well.

Trauma has a profound effect on learning. The ability to think critically, focus intently, and handle one's emotions and impulses can all be greatly impacted by adverse traumatic events in a child's life.

When we bring children into our home and remove them from the situations that have brought much of the trauma into their lives, it is the first step to helping them learn. We have to be alert and involved in their education to make sure their learning needs are being met. Develop relationships with those in their learning environment to work together on the best action that will benefit them.

Another thing to consider is whether the learning environment is a stressful one. Does your child get the help they need to excel? Is this environment

complimentary to neurodiverse learners? Are they valued
as a person? Do they enjoy learning? Does the structure
of the learning environment work for them, or against
them? These questions can determine if a change is
needed.

*"Scientists have recently determined that it takes
approximately 400 repetitions to create a new synapse in
the brain – unless it is done with play, in which case, it
takes between 10 and 20 repetitions!"*
Dr. Karyn Purvis

My Sensational Six represent a wide range of giftedness
and special needs. Among my crew, we have reading
challenges (Dyslexia), math challenges (Dyscalculia),
writing challenges (Dysgraphia), sensory challenges
(SPD), and attention deficits (ADD and ADHD). We
don't allow labels to define our children. This is one of
the many reasons why our style of learning is interest-led
and focused on hands-on exploration. What I love about
this learning environment is that it squashes all
perceptions of what a person can or cannot do.

*"Kids who have experienced trauma have difficulty
learning unless they feel safe and supported."*
Caelan Kuban Soma

One of my children has a challenge with calculation and
math concepts. It has always been a struggle. Her gifting
is so strong in other areas, we would be negligent to
ignore it. We expose her to all the basics for the direction
that she desires to go. However, we focus more on
strengths, dreams, and potential. Learning through their
interests allows us to do that.

Another child struggles with the ability to write fluently. The connection between their brilliant thoughts and the page is a painful (physical and mental) process. They have no shortage of stories or information to share. We make sure that they have other tools to express their brilliance to the world like typing, voice-to-text software, and dictation. It restores confidence in a learning atmosphere that does not see challenges as a roadblock.

> *"What I love about this learning environment is that it squashes all perceptions of what a person can or cannot do."*

Trauma and Learning

I have found that this learning environment is particularly effective with children who have suffered traumatic events in their lives. Trauma can affect a child's ability to learn and grow in a traditional learning environment. In the line of work that I'm in, I have seen many children misdiagnosed as ADHD, when in fact they had PTSD. This was as a result of early childhood trauma which affected all aspects of their lives. Both conditions present similarly in behavior and testing.

For example, a child who struggles with ADHD or emotional regulation can perfect a skill and interest with pride while having the room to work on their challenges. Approaching it this way brings confidence and the ability to be highlighted for their strengths, instead of weaknesses.

That is what I want for all of my children. Giftedness or not, special needs or not, I want them to see themselves as valued, talented, and full of potential.

Beautiful Moments

I will never forget the times when my children have mastered something they worked extremely hard at. The look on their face from accomplishing something that once seemed impossible is a beautiful moment. These moments happened because they had the time and environment that allowed them to move at their own pace.

What I Have Learned

I learned not to underestimate the effects of trauma on the brain, or to underestimate how much a supportive and compassionate learning environment can make all the difference in the confidence of the child.

Prayer

God, I ask you to guide me to the perfect school, program, and teachers that will value my child and their potential. Thank you for blessing them with a learning environment and instructors with patience, compassion, and inspiration to do their best.

In Jesus' Name,
Amen

"An adoptee's curiosity about one's past is not a rejection of one's present nor a sign of unhappiness or dysfunction. It's exploring what should be the adoptee's already…knowledge of one's personal history and family members."

Tara Vanderwoude

Chapter 17
In Their Own Words

*O*ver the years I have come to recognize how important the voice of the adoptee and foster alumni are. For too long the adoption narrative has been controlled by "experts" and adoptive parents. The most important person in the equation of adoption and foster care is the child.

I have spent the last several years opening my eyes and ears to their voices to reprogram myself and those I come in contact with. When I opened myself up to hear things that are hard, I stepped into their stories and decided to be a change agent in any way I could.

This has also impacted my parenting as an adoptive parent. It is easy to operate on parenting autopilot and not consider how it has affected the psyche, self-esteem, and narrative of my child's story.

It is a right of the adoptee and the foster youth to know who they are and where they come from. It should not in any way offend us to support their curiosity and possible reunification. Our confidence as those who love them should be in the relationship we have fostered over the time we have had with them. Part of the healing process for many includes finding and understanding the details of those who gave them life and all the perspectives connected to the separation of their families.

You may have some who are not interested in searching for and reuniting with their first families. That is okay.

Allow them to approach their story in their way, in their time. Our goal as adoptive and foster parents is to be supportive of healing and closure for them. That can look differently for every person.

They have to know that you are there, supportive, and that you have their back no matter how the reunification goes. We all want to think it will be a fairy tale ending, and for some it is. However, it is a painful process for all involved that drudges up old wounds that are not easy to revisit. Be patient with your kids. Simply BE THERE.

I have gathered three amazing women who were brave enough to share their story in hopes that it will give you a glimpse into their world and a fresh look at the children in your care. Their stories have not been altered. Their stories are **In Their Own Words**.

Heidi's Story (48) - Who Am I?

My mom had two large decorative wall mirrors hanging above our plastic-covered sofa in the living room. I remember pulling my face up to the mirrors and peering in as I examined my face. I was searching for her face, my sister's face, something that looked like them. I couldn't find them in my face, nor my face in theirs.

As early as nine years old, I struggled with feeling like I didn't really belong. I didn't understand these feelings for years. My mom would often say to me, "You know your mother is white." I would look at her brown-sugared complexion and wonder what she was talking about. One day she asked, "Do you know where your name Heidi

Elizabeth came from?" I said excitedly, "Yes! You named me Heidi after your favorite Shirley Temple movie!" That made perfect sense to me because my sister's name was Shirley. Sundays before church we'd watch old black and white Shirley Temple films.

My mom was a divorcee. I grew up with my older sister who had Down Syndrome, and my brother who was already grown and out of the house. As I went through childhood, I was often confused by my extended family's side eyes and hushed conversations at holiday gatherings. I was brought up in California by an African American family with Southern roots. Thanksgiving was a time when aunties and older cousins had conversations in the kitchen. They would always get silent when children were in earshot. I recall hearing my aunts and older cousins saying, "How is Bill's daughter doing?" or "Do you think Heidi will end up like her mother?" I was so puzzled, because my mom was great, hard-working and beautiful. What did they mean "...end up like her mother"? I went to private school, got good grades...why wouldn't they want me to be like my mom? Adding to my confusion was the fact that my dad's name wasn't Bill.

I would stare intently at my cousins' faces, searching for who I looked like and, sometimes, I would think I saw something. I have an olive complexion and long hair like my cousin Dorian, but it was like Goldilocks and the three bears: it just wasn't the perfect fit. Strangely, I would gaze at the singer Cher or the actress Jennifer Beal and wonder "Is that my mother?" I would shake it off because that made no sense. My mom was my mom, right?

There is a vivid memory that makes me laugh to this day. I was about thirteen or fourteen years old when my mom was on the phone with her bedroom door closed. Now, everyone knows that when mom's door is closed, she is talking about something juicy. I pressed my ear to the door and listened. I could hear low tones of her talking and made out something about ADOPTION—I was ecstatic! Was she adopting a baby!?! In that moment, it never occurred to me that she was talking about me.

Fast forward to June 1989, as I readied for high school graduation and made the final decision to enlist into the US Army. My mom sat me down and showed me my birth certificate. In the mother and father boxes were names that I didn't recognize. She explained that she was my aunt, and my sister and brother were actually my cousins. I was her brother's child. He passed away and my biological mother was out there somewhere. I was shocked. My mom was a matter of fact type of person, and there were no dramatics—she told me because I would see the birth certificate when I enlisted. That was it. Nothing more…no questions answered or allowed to be asked.

As the years passed, I would bravely ask questions and would get short, vague answers. I heard things like, "She is German or Jewish or something", "She was a young runaway on drugs", "Your father was a good man." My aunt once said that in the first six months of her having me, I would reach for any Caucasian woman who resembled my biological mother. Yes, she looked like Cher. I came to realize that I resided with my biological parents until around the age of two or three years old. I was deeply affected by the fact that I had no recollection of my parents. This affected my decisions once I became a single parent in the military. I refused duty assignments that would restrict me from bringing my son. I didn't want him to forget me, like I forgot my parents.

At certain milestones in my life, I would comb the White Pages for my mother, making phone calls, ending up with no answers. Once my aunt fell ill to cancer, she would blurt out horrible things about my biological mother's treatment of me. Nonetheless, my resolve was always, "She loved me enough to leave me." I grew up in a nice suburb and went to private school. What kind of life would I have had with her, a young runaway who was a drug addict? There was always something missing; no explanation for my looks or history. Before my aunt's passing, she formally adopted me. She wanted to make sure I was in her will, and no one could contest what she wanted for me. I was twenty-six years old.

About five years ago, on a whim, I Googled her name. I FOUND HER! It was a bittersweet moment. It was her obituary. She had gotten her life together and had been married for over twenty-five years. She was loved and respected in her community. She was a mere six-hour drive from me, and I had missed her by no more than a year. It was so funny because, through the years, I would often say that I could pass my biological mother on the street and would never know it was her.

I then Googled her father's name. My grandfather was alive and living in Philadelphia. I called and left my name on his machine. Hours ticked by while I waited with bated breath. Then the phone rang, late Sunday evening. The Caller ID read the family name. It was my uncle, my mother's brother who lived about forty-five minutes away from my Georgia home. We exchanged information and he vetted me through dates and location. He recalled when his sister ran away and the times she had called home. He asked, "Do you know how you got your middle name?" I said no. He explained that in Jewish tradition, you are named for a loved one that has passed on. "Your grandmother's name was Ellen, so your mother named you Elizabeth. I know for sure you are my sister's daughter." I told him I was biracial and he said that made no difference to him. About a week later, my grandfather called.

The voice that was on the line was shaky, raspy, and guarded. He asked pointed questions about where I was from and how I grew up. He was obviously cautious and plainly stated that, "Sheri never mentioned you at all." By getting to know my grandfather and posting the journey on social media, I met people who knew my mother and father before I was born. I learned that the picture that had been painted of my parents was not entirely true. My biological parents loved each other as best they could. She was sixteen, he was forty-eight. It was the 70s, the time of peace, love, and Woodstock. Sheri wasn't equipped to be anyone's mother and Bill thought the best thing to do was ask if one of his sisters would take his baby in. I was told later that after my father passed away, my mother tried to get me back from my aunt. My aunt was formidable to this young woman.

My uncle shared with me that my biological mother's husband always felt that she was longing for someone from her past. Sadly, this longing wasn't strong enough for her to mention my existence to anyone, even on her deathbed. To this day, that still haunts me, even though my uncle and grandfather have come to love and accept me. Finding my biological mother's family has filled in pieces of the puzzle that complete me. I am able to give my children a bit of fullness of who they are because I have a better understanding of who I am. Now, I look fondly at the only two pictures I have of my mother. One was when she was young. My firstborn son looks exactly like her. After meeting my uncle in person, he wept, saying, "You are the spitting image of my sister." As we have gotten to know each other, he often remarks that my sense of humor and quick wit is "all Sheri." At the same time, my biological father's side of the family say, "You are certainly Bill's daughter." My aunt really never wanted me to know that I wasn't hers. Her selflessness and love have made me hers, and she will always be my mom.

This journey has allowed me to find parts of me that I never knew I was missing. As for my biological mother's family, they too have healed from wounds that they thought were buried with their daughter. Me, I am still healing, learning, and growing.

Tiana's Story (48) - Something Is Missing?

I've always known that I was adopted. It would be hard not to since my parents are Caucasian. As a child of transracial adoption in the early 1970s, it was unusual to see a black child with white parents. I'm sure that there were people who saw us and wondered what was going on. Why would they have a black child? Why not a white child?

There were family members who were not exactly on board with "mixing races." I heard that my great-grandfather was not a fan of "blacks." He was outwardly prejudiced. However, he was okay with me. My dad thinks it was because I was an infant. I couldn't hurt him, or whatever else he thought someone with my skin color would do to him. I think my winning personality and smile as an infant were too much for the man.

I was born in Detroit, Michigan and was adopted at four months old. I remember seeing in my baby book a piece of paper that had my schedule written on it. It showed my eating schedule, my sleeping schedule, and whatever else my foster mom thought my parents should know about me. I remember Mom saying that I was sleeping through the night when they brought me home.

When I was about three years old, my parents adopted my sister from Vietnam. She is Vietnamese and African American. When I was about seven, my parents adopted my brother from Saginaw, Michigan. I remember being able to see his picture in this booklet of children available for adoption. It was like picking something out from a catalog. In my mind, it was neat that we could see photos of him before we met him. It was so different than when my parents adopted me, as they had no idea what I looked like until the day they came to pick me up from my foster mother.

I grew up without anyone who was biologically connected to me in my family. For some adoptees, that is hard. It didn't occur to me that this was different in some way. I didn't see my siblings differently because we weren't related by DNA. I feel like I had some of the typical sibling experiences that biologically connected siblings have—arguments over seating in the car, sharing a room with my sister, or whose turn it is to do certain chores.

As I grew up, I never thought about my birth parents much. Sometimes I would think about my birth mom and wonder how many children she had after she had me. I really had it all figured out in my head about how life probably had turned out for her. Here's how my version of the story went. She was really young when she had me, which is why she placed me for adoption. She eventually got married, had a few more children, and was living a good life. I sometimes wondered if she thought about me, but I figured that she wouldn't because we both had good lives that we were living. The end.

That is not how the story went at all. Not that I had ever planned on finding out. I had no plans of finding my birth mom, let alone my birth father, or any siblings. I remember being asked about it when I was in high school. I said that I hadn't thought about doing it and probably wouldn't. In my mind, the woman who gave birth to me was just that—the woman who gave birth to me, not my mom. I had a mom already and there was nothing that I thought she could bring to the table. I did not feel there was something to gain from meeting her.

While in college, a friend of mine connected with her birth mom, and it wasn't smooth sailing. My friend was an adult and had established her life. Trying to figure out how she was going to integrate this new person into her life was harder than she anticipated. Actually, she hadn't thought about those dynamics when she moved forward with the reunion. How could one know that? There were no resources available in the late 1980s to help adoptees walk through a reunification process.

Hearing about her experience was an added exclamation point in my mind. I was not interested in connecting with anyone biologically related to me. I had a life. I liked my life as it was. I didn't want to figure out how to change my life around. Someone who had not been part of my world now wanted to possibly monopolize all of it. No thanks. I'm good.

I want to explain that being adopted is great, but it is not without its own challenges. Most people think that as long as the child is in a good, stable home that there's nothing more to think about. Oh, contraire mon frere!

Many people are not aware of the trauma that comes with adoption. "How is there trauma?" "Were you abused in some way?" The unrecognized trauma is called abandonment or in some cases involves PTSD—Post-Traumatic Stress Disorder. Now, there can be other trauma that is experienced by an adoptee due to so many factors. However, at the basic level, a child's birth family left them. It's a basic fact, regardless of the circumstances. It sounds harsh when you say it. That's the reality. I didn't even realize that I was experiencing issues with abandonment. It wasn't until six months before the opportunity to connect with my birth mother that I recognized something was amiss.

In the 1970s, adoption agencies and even the world of psychology, particularly for early childhood development, were not as knowledgeable of the impact of this separation from their birth family. Even when the situation warranted it, the child was forever marked by that moment. It wasn't until I was well into adulthood that I even realized that I was marked by this loss. I never felt it consciously. As I look back over my life, I see the impact as I tried to be the person everyone would like and want to be around. If I didn't, there was a fear of abandonment. The subconscious question in my head was, "What do I need to do to make you stay?" Today there are many resources made available and strongly encouraged for adoptive families to help with trauma and transition. There are also more resources available to families experiencing transracial and international adoptions than there were when I was born.

My parents were intentional about my siblings and me being around people who looked like us and having various cultural experiences. However, I was not prepared for people to view me as less than. I think there were situations that would have been hard, had I been on my own. Having my parents there, I was accepted. I could pass. Living on my own as an adult and navigating the world without the protection of my parents' white privilege, there were times that I was naïve about the atmosphere around me. If there was something I could add, it would be that piece—to know how to navigate in a world that is not always welcoming toward people of color.

When I received a phone call in late January of 2018, I was quite taken by surprise that my birth mother wanted to connect. It never occurred to me that she or anyone who was biologically related to me could petition the court to have a confidential intermediary locate me. Since my birth records are sealed, that's the only way that either one of us could find the other. I hadn't planned on this possibility, so I wasn't prepared with an answer. I wasn't prepared for anything.

I have to admit that I was angry initially. This was interrupting my life! I didn't ask for her to reach out to me! I didn't ask for her to hire someone to find me! Next came the reasons to say no to the request. She would try to take over my life. How was I going to really fit her into my life? She probably would want to monopolize all of my time. The list goes on. They were all things that were totally beyond my control.

I made a special trip to see my parents to discuss the situation. They were very supportive. At the end of the day, whatever decision I made, they were going to be there for me. If I chose to connect with my birth mom or if I chose not to, they were okay. They knew that it didn't change my relationship with them. They would always be my parents. This is critical because some adoptees do not have this support from their family. We need to know that our parents don't view us as being disloyal or rejecting them. The reason that this is important is because we are walking into the unknown. What may look like a positive experience initially can change at any point, leaving another rejection notice. Knowing that our parents are there for the bumpy landings is so helpful.

After almost three weeks of processing, I made the decision to connect with my birth mom. I opted to start with email and go from there. It was bumpy at first, but we kept at it. The emails eventually connected me to my half-brother. He started emailing me. It wasn't long before we exchanged phone numbers and were talking on the phone almost daily. The connection with him was like someone I had known all my life but hadn't spoken with in a long time.

My version of how my birth mom's life played out was much different. The real story is that I was her second child. I had a brother who was about two-and-a-half years older than myself. She made the decision to go into the military. She said that she was only allowed to bring one child with her on the base. Being about nineteen or twenty, she had to make a choice. The little girl in me says, "Why didn't you pick something else?" The adult in me, who has been able to interact with her, knows. With her personality, I know that the person I am today would not have been able to blossom. When someone is overly critical, it stumps the growth of everyone around them. God knew what I was going to need, even before I was born.

In May of 2018, my brother came from Birmingham, Alabama to see me. It was an emotional reunion. I was fortunate enough to have a friend capture it on video. That July, I flew to Memphis, Tennessee to visit my birth mom for the first time. This was another emotional reunion. It's one thing to communicate via phone and email, quite another to see each other in person. "What will they think of me when they see me?" "Will she be angry with me for giving her up?" "Will she think my parents did a good job raising me?" It really could go in a myriad of directions, so everyone is cautiously optimistic.

It was during the visit to Memphis that I was given what was believed to be the address for my birth father. I sat on the address for about ten months. Then one morning, during my devotions, God made it clear that I needed to write a letter to him that day. Tearfully, I wrote the brief, one-page letter letting him know who I was. I was hoping he would want to connect with me.

A week later, I had an email from his wife that he did want to connect. In July of 2019, I drove to Detroit, Michigan and met him for the first time. Meeting and getting to know him has been one of the best things for me. In meeting him, I felt like missing pieces fell into place, pieces that I didn't even know were missing! These were parts of who I am, where I come from, and my identity that have been imprinted on my heart from the very beginning. It's something that adoption cannot change (nature). The person I became because of my adoptive parents (nurture) cannot be changed by connecting with my biological family. All the pieces of the puzzle were connected.

Agnes' Story (23) - A Whole New World

I had the pleasure of interviewing Agnes about her story of adoption. It was an absolute pleasure learning about her life and how she came to the US. The series of questions and answers came from our discussion and are sure to be a blessing to you.

The Beginning
Agnes is now a twenty-three-year-old college student in the United States. However, life began thousands of miles away in Uganda. She was the newborn daughter to her mother and father, who were in their teens. Her mom came from a Muslim family that lived in the city. Her mother's parents valued education and invested greatly in their daughter's future. A baby was not part of the plan.

Agnes' father was born into a Christian family of farmers in the countryside. They were hard-working people and trained their son to be the same. A baby was not part of the plan.

Their vastly different worlds and religions were a firestorm that made their love and hope of being a family impossible. This eventually tore them apart. As her mother went her way and attempted to raise Agnes on her own, things did not go as planned. She was shunned by her family for ruining her future education.

As Agnes looks back, she often felt that her mother blamed her for ruining her plans for her life. This led to Agnes being shifted between several homes of friends and family. She eventually landed in her great-grandmother's home around the age of five. The ages and dates are not clear because Agnes never celebrated birthdays. Agnes' mother gave birth to her younger brother by the same father, and he was a sickly child. Her great-grandmother later fell ill and was no longer able to take care of Agnes. While her brother Fred stayed with his mother, Agnes was sent to live at an orphanage where she also attended school.

The Orphanage

Agnes was at the orphanage from the ages of seven to fourteen. It was dormitory-style living with very few amenities. There were approximately 600 children at that time. Because she was one of the oldest children at the orphanage, she was required to help care for the rest of the children. Her days were filled with schooling and chores, such as washing everyone's clothes, cooking, cleaning, and looking after the little ones. Eventually, Agnes' brother Fred and two cousins joined her at the orphanage. She was fully responsible for caring for them, even though she was a child herself.

She has mixed feelings about the orphanage. Fighting for food and fending for themselves, many children did not know what it was like to have their needs met. For most of her life, it was all she knew. There was very little exposure to the outside world. Agnes did not know that life was any different on the outside until she started venturing off on holidays. Her mother and other family members would come pick her up from time to time.

Often, Americans would come with toys, candy, clothes, and promises of a better life. Many of the children hung on to their every word, only to never see them again. They felt that white people were superior and that all Americans must be rich. It was a revolving door of visitors that compounded the trauma in the hearts of the kids at the orphanage.

Agnes remembers watching children pray for families. She had never heard of adoption before. It was not until a very close friend suddenly disappeared. She later saw a picture of her with her new family in America, and that was when she recognized the meaning of adoption. Whenever kids were matched with a new family, they were instructed not to share the news with the other children. Agnes would soon learn more about adoption.

Jodi and her oldest daughter were admonished to visit the orphanage on a trip to Uganda in 2009. Jodi explained that she and her husband were looking to adopt two children. The orphanage director mentioned that she had three children that needed to be adopted together. That was Agnes and her two cousins. Jodi agreed to meet the trio in anticipation.

Adoption
One day, Agnes was pulled from her day classes to join the director and Jodi in the guest house, along with her cousins. Agnes had no idea why she was there and was confused. Jodi shared pictures of her family and her life in the United States. The kids were still confused as to how that related to them.

Jodi finally said to them that she wanted them to become part of her family. She wanted to be their mom. Agnes' cousins were immediately in agreement, but Agnes was not quite convinced. She had been promised forever by a lot of people in her life. She was not interested in more heartache. After a walk with Jodi, Agnes told Jodi, "I will only agree if you promise me this is FOREVER." Jodi promised, and the process of adoption began.

At this time, Agnes' brother went to live with his aunt. She was told by the orphanage director to not mention her brother, Fred. The director felt it would complicate things for the adoption of the other three. Even though she did not understand, Agnes obeyed the instruction.

A New Life
By October 2010, Agnes (15) and her cousins, now her siblings, arrived in the US. A short time after, her brother Fred joined them as the newest addition to the family in 2013. Jodi and her husband now had a huge family, including their biological children from previous marriages, an older adopted daughter and four new adopted children from Uganda. They were one big happy family.

The transition to life in the United States was anything but easy or smooth. The hardest part for Agnes was allowing someone else to take care of her. She had always been the oldest and had spent her life taking care of herself and other children. Now she was a middle child. Understanding what it was like to have parents and have someone take care of all of your needs was a new concept.

Agnes spent a lot of time parenting and instructing her younger siblings like she always had. Trusting her new parents to care for her siblings was something that had to be earned. Eventually they earned her trust and she let go of the responsibility that a child should never have had.

Outside of the newness of living in a family, Agnes was overwhelmed by all the things that were completely foreign to her, like paved roads, water, and electricity at her fingertips, a closet full of clothes and shoes, and food in abundance.

She found it hard to relate to other kids in school. The language barrier and cultural differences were a great change from what she was used to. Agnes found herself being bullied. She often had questions about her skin color and felt the need to grow her hair, just to fit in. In Uganda, boys and girls wore their hair short for health reasons.

Agnes felt her adoptive parents helped her adjust to her new life by sheltering them in the beginning and exposing them to new things slowly. They made sure that she and her siblings had a routine like they were used to. Her new parents were very open to talking and helping them through the tough emotions as they arose.

Today
Agnes has a lot of feelings and experiences to unpack when making sense of her life. She says that surrounding herself with family helped her get through some very rough times. Finding someone she could trust and talk to about her childhood experiences was a key to healing. It

took her several therapists before she found the right fit. Agnes agrees that healing takes time and evolves throughout your life.

After six years in the US, Agnes reconnected with her biological family. She talks with her mother periodically and tries to send financial assistance when she can. Her relationship with her father is not very strong. She feels her biological parents are more like friends than parents. Agnes has lots of questions that have never been answered but has resolved to move forward. She offers forgiveness and no longer harbors bitterness toward them. Agnes feels that her experiences have affected her ability to trust people. She has also found that it has affected her comfort level when it comes to relating to men. This is a constant struggle that she is working on.

Agnes has advice for foster and adoptive parents that will help them to be the best for their kids.

- Know that adoption is not easy.
- Don't do it if you have doubts.
- Get as much training as you can and take advantage of all of the available resources.
- Know that there is no way to be 100% prepared.
- Know as much about their stories in advance as you possibly can.
- Recognize it takes time for kids to open up—if they ever open up.
- It takes time to get to know your child.
- There is no one-size-fits-all parenting method.
- Don't give up on them when they push you away.
- There will be a lot of emotional growth for the parent and the child.

Beautiful Moments

With all three of the ladies who shared their stories, there were many beautiful moments. The one that strikes me the most is the self-actualization that unfolded as they sought truth, connected with biological family, and embraced forgiveness.

What I Have Learned

As an adoptive parent and a child advocate, I have learned so much from the stories of these amazing women. One of the most impacted things that I learned was the need to be intentional and purposeful in my role as a healing agent for my kids.

Prayer

Lord, thank you for the ability to be a witness in the lives of the children you have placed in my care. I pray for wisdom, direction, and resources to give them what they need to be all that you have called them to be. Father, help me to be intentional in my parenting and advocacy. Give me insight into their needs and stories to guide them through tough emotions and seasons in their lives. Let me be the healing agent that you have called me to be for them.

In Jesus' Name,
Amen

"It is not you against this child. It is YOU and YOUR CHILD against your child's history. It is not a personal attack on you."

Dr. Karyn Purvis

Chapter 18
No Matter What...

By exercising the principles in this book, we have seen healing, growth, changes in behavior, and a strong relationship with our children. Intentionality and prayer will help you to build that bond with your kids that you always wanted.

> *"I have never met a child who can't come to deep levels of healing."*
> *Dr. Karyn Purvis*

Only God

No matter how much you do as a parent to nurture, love, and provide for your children, there is a place you cannot fill for them. The separation from their family, no matter how recent or distant, leaves a hole, questions, and wondering you cannot answer for them.

Your children are only going to find the help they need in God. Their unanswered questions, the missing puzzle pieces, and the healing they need comes from Him. My heart aches when I see my children searching for companionship, friendship, popularity, esteem, and significance in all the wrong places. I am committed to consistently redirecting them back to the source. No person, job, or amount of money can fill the hole that only God can fill in their lives. Only GOD!!

Throughout this book you have noticed the theme NO MATTER WHAT...

This is because the commitment to a child must be forever. The love must be unconditional. The prayer must be fervent. The advocacy must be bold. The guidance must be intentional. The desire to be a healing agent must be purposeful. The trauma competency must be continual. Through thick and thin, good and bad, hard and simple, pain and healing, NO MATTER WHAT!!!

Prayer

Father, I pray that you cover my children and that trauma has no root in their soul. I thank you that they will look toward Heaven, from where their help comes, and find joy, answers, and stability. I pray they find a friend closer than a brother in your arms, dear God. Let their lives honor you. Let their testimony bring praise to your faithfulness, healing, and power to restore. Let them use the gifts and talents you gave them for you. Protect them, Lord. Remind them of your word that was sown in their hearts. Bring peace to their minds and hearts.

In Jesus' Name,
Amen

Author's Work

Homeschool Gone Wild
Inspired Learning through Living

Mom ~ Spiration
Inspire Your Children to Pursue Their Dreams as
You Pursue Your Own

Let Go!
A Control Freak's Fight for Peace

No Matter What...
Fighting for Kids through the Tough Stuff of
Foster Care and Adoption

Now What?
What Do I Do When My Kid

Loses Their Way?

Connect with Karla

Facebook
Karla and the Sensational Six
BeBold Publishing

Instagram
Karla and the Sensational 6

YouTube
Karla and the Sensational Six

Website
www.karlamariewilliams.com
www.BoldPublisher.com

Resources

The Connected Child by Dr. Karyn Purvis
www.empoweredtoconnect.org

The Great Behavior Breakdown by Bryan Post
From Fear to Love by Bryan Post
www.postinstitute.com

When Your Kid Is Hurting by Dr. Leman

The Five Love Languages of Children by Gary Chapman

Calming Angry Kids by Tricia Goyer

Triggers by Amber Lia & Wendy Speake

The Foster Parenting Toolbox by EMK Press

Let Go! By Karla Marie Williams
Now What? By Karla Marie Williams
www.KarlaMarieWilliams.com

Made in the USA
Las Vegas, NV
04 November 2020